Fixing or changing the pattern?

Reflections on widening adult participation in learning

Fixing or changing the pattern?

Reflections on widening adult participation in learning

Veronica McGivney

NIACE
THE NATIONAL ORGANISATION
FOR ADULT LEARNING

Published by the
National Institute of Adult Continuing Education (England and Wales)
21 De Montfort Street
Leicester LE1 7GE

Company registration no. 2603322
Charity registration no. 1002775

First published 2001
© 2001 National Institute of Adult Continuing Education (England and
Wales)

NIACE, the national organisation for adult learning, has a broad remit to
promote lifelong learning opportunities for adults. NIACE works to
develop increased participation in education and training, particularly for
those who do not have easy access because of barriers of class, gender, age,
race, language and culture, learning difficulties and disabilities, or
insufficient financial resources.

NIACE's website on the internet is http://www.niace.org.uk

ISBN 1-86201-122-2

Cataloguing in Publications Data
A CIP record for this title is available from the British Library

Cover design by: Brooke Calverley
Designed and typeset by Boldface, London EC1
Printed and bound in Great Britain by Hobbs

Contents

Acknowledgements vi
Foreword vii

1 Introduction 1

2 Identifying the pattern 13

What has fixed the pattern?

3 Policy factors 33

4 Supply and institutional factors 51

5 Personal and cultural factors 69

How to change the pattern

6 Lessons from practice 79

7 The impact of current policy 108

8 Revising assumptions and strategies 131

9 Final thoughts 149

References 165

Acknowledgements

Sincere thanks are due to the DfEE (as it then was) for supporting this study; to my NIACE Research and Development colleagues who contributed thoughts and information from their own work; and, especially, to the following for so readily giving up some of their valuable time in order to be interviewed: Alan Tuckett, Bob Fryer, Dan Taubman, Ed Ellis, Judith Summers, Leisha Fullick, Margaret Davey and Martin Yarnit.

Many thanks also to my colleagues Andy Kail for patiently hunting down articles and references, Sue Parkins for her constant help and support throughout, and Alan Tuckett for his helpful comments on the text.

Foreword

In writing *Fixing or Changing the Pattern?* I have drawn on my own research over the last 12 years, the extensive literature on participation and related topics, the work and views of my NIACE colleagues, and the perceptions and experiences of some key people who have been working in the field during the period spanned by the book and who were kind enough to agree to be interviewed. Quotations from these people are attributed to 'interviewees'. Quotations from colleagues and other informants who were not interviewed but who contributed thoughts and ideas from their experience are attributed to 'informants'.

Chapter 1

Introduction

Eleven years ago NIACE published the findings of some ESRC-funded research I had conducted on adult participation in education, under the title *Education's for Other People* (McGivney, 1990). Conducted at a time of rapid change, when new legislation – the Education Reform Act – was about to alter the regulations and structures of post-16 education and training (a situation very similar to the one we have recently re-experienced), the study revealed persisting class, age and occupational divisions between participants and non-participants in organised learning. It also showed that there were wide variations between further and higher education institutions, local education authorities and other providers in the extent and nature of the efforts they were making to attract and work with the sizeable groups who were not taking advantage of organised learning opportunities.

The research showed that while some educational organisations and institutions had made considerable progress in working with hitherto neglected sections of the population, others had done little and any attempts to change mainstream practices were fiercely resisted. Several times I was told that as education centres and institutions and the programmes they offered were 'open' to all members of the community, no special measures needed to be taken to facilitate the participation of the groups most conspicuously under-represented. In other words, the failure of the latter to avail themselves of the opportunities available was the result of their own inertia or lack of motivation rather than of any problems they experienced, any shortcomings on the part of the provider or any unsuitable aspects of the courses available. As a result, participation in the courses and programmes organised by these providers remained the preserve of middle-class and higher educated people – a learner profile that typified participants in most organised forms of post-compulsory learning at the time.

The aim of the present study was to consider what, if any, changes have occurred in the intervening decade. Is education still perceived to be 'for other people' or have we made any progress towards enabling a broader mix of the population to participate in organised learning opportunities? What lessons have we learned about how to engage people in learning and what do we still need to know and do? Can the Government's aim of increasing demand for learning among those who engage in it least be achieved?

The establishment in 2001 of a new framework for post-compulsory learning makes this an opportune moment to consider these questions.

Historical antecedents

The concern with opening up learning opportunities to wider sections of the community is far from new, although 'widening participation' is a relatively recent term:

> *The history of adult education as a 'movement' and the social purposes which have often motivated its practitioners means that there has always been a drive, at least on the part of some, to bring into education and training the 'missing groups'.* (Hillage et al, 2000: 82)

Some date this back to university initiatives in the 18th century to make lectures available to the wider population or to the university extension mission of the 19th century (Ward and Steele, 1999). In the first half of the 20th century there were sporadic enquiries into adult attitudes to and participation in education (ACACE (1982) refers to surveys dated 1936 and 1953). Such investigations became more frequent after the 1960s when a series of studies and surveys confirmed that post-compulsory education services were chiefly benefiting younger, better educated and higher income groups. Among these one can note *Adequacy of Provision* (NIAE 1970), the Russell enquiry undertaken for the then Department of Education and Science (Russell, 1973), Peter Clyne's influential report *The Disadvantaged Adult* (Clyne, 1972), and the series of surveys undertaken by the Advisory Council for Adult and Continuing Education (ACACE).

Between the 1960s and 1980s there was a number of important initiatives designed to make post-compulsory learning opportunities more accessible and attractive to those who for a variety of reasons were unable or unwilling to participate in existing provision. The Open University was established; a nationwide basic skills campaign was launched, and a range of new learner-centred, community-based programmes including, notably, 'Return to Learn' and 'Second Chance' courses, were developed for working-class communities, people without qualifications, the unemployed, women and minority ethnic groups. During the same period, outreach programmes and action research projects designed to encourage working-class communities to define and achieve their own learning requirements were being developed in cities such as Leeds, Liverpool and Southampton, by radical adult educationists concerned with the social purpose of education.

Alongside these developments, some further education colleges and adult education centres, the adult residential colleges, the Workers' Educational Association and other voluntary organisations were working, as now, to provide learning opportunities for many of the groups neglected by other parts of the system.

One of the most effective drives to change the traditional adult learner profile took place in London after evidence provided for the Russell enquiry had revealed stark class, income and racial disparities in participation. Following the recommendations of a special working party set up in the wake of that enquiry, the Inner London Education Authority (ILEA) appointed a team of community education workers to conduct outreach activities in working-class communities and local estates, and the adult education institutes adopted a number of strategies to recruit the most excluded groups. These included establishing a strong learner-centred ethos and implementing a very low fee policy. This approach succeeded in creating a culture of learning among people hitherto neglected by learning providers:

> *It was part of London's culture to go to classes. You got working-class people, black people, young women doing all sorts of things, evening classes, and in the day. We invented loads of things – in ILEA and elsewhere – in those days: family workshops, adult literacy, working with the unemployed, working with women, Access and Return to Learn, community activists. We provided the momentum, the models and the people. The underlying principle was that if you did nothing, the class system would discriminate against people, therefore you had to do something to avoid that bias. We knew we had to start where people were at and be sensitive to their lives. The purpose was community involvement and individual empowerment.* (Interviewee)

According to Uden (1996), ILEA was:

> *one of the first organisations to grasp the key fact that the expansion of participation which took place in the fifties and sixties had not effectively widened participation beyond those who were traditional or habitual learners and had then done something about it.* (p33)

Although ILEA was dismantled in 1990, producing a serious set-back to the progress made in widening participation in the capital, other developments took place nationally that helped to continue some of the momentum towards more equitable access. These included the further development of Access courses to prepare adults for entry to higher education; the expansion of Open College Networks offering flexible accreditation for programmes designed to respond to the needs of specific groups of learners; the establishment of the National Open College Network (NOCN) and the first Credit Accumulation and Transfer agreement on which its constitution was based. Assisted by these developments as well as by new qualification routes and more flexible entrance arrangements, delivery mechanisms and learning modes, the number of mature students, especially women and members of some ethnic minority groups, increased rapidly in both the further and higher education sectors:

> *As FE went increasingly into access work with mature students, new groups with new support needs came to the fore. Colleges increasingly took over responsibilities that were previously the responsibilities of a small group of niche-market institutions such as residential colleges.* (Interviewee)

However, many of the initiatives which originated in an aspiration to facilitate the engagement of new adult learners succeeded largely in reaching more of the same:

> *from the founding of the public schools to the development of the WEA, the most affluent members of society have benefited from initiatives intended for the least.* (Woodrow, 2001: 9)

The Open University, for example,

> *despite its heroic commitment to wider social participation and student choice, soaked up demand for higher education principally from the financially solvent, professionalised but credentially impoverished middle-class.* (Robertson, 1997a:12)

Thus, although many of the developments of the 1970s and 1980s succeeded in bringing more and different adult learners into post-16 education programmes, they did not significantly alter the social class composition of the *overall* adult learner body. National surveys, the findings of which were summarised in *Education's for Other People* (McGivney, 1990), indicated that the socio-economic profile of learners engaging in education and training programmes remained largely unchanged throughout the 1980s and at the beginning of the 1990s, and it was shortly after this time that the term 'widening participation' began increasingly to be used.

The recent preoccupation with widening participation is therefore based on the persistent finding that, although participation in post-compulsory learning has been expanding, the expansion has largely involved students from the same social background as before. During the 1990s, successive national surveys revealed an enduring pattern: large numbers of adults had not taken part in any organised learning since leaving school and there was a clear 'learning divide' linked to age, qualifications, occupation and social class (see Chapter 2).

In the early 1990s, it was not so much a concern for social justice that led to widening participation becoming a key policy objective, but fears about low qualification levels and declining economic competitiveness. Part of the remit of the Further Education Funding Council, established by the 1992 Further and Higher Education Act, was to promote access to further education: 'for people who do not participate in education and training but who could benefit from it' and the Kennedy Committee on widening participation was set up to advise the Council on how to achieve that aim. Education and training targets were also introduced to encourage publicly-funded education providers to widen participation as part of their core mission. After the election of a new Labour Government in 1997, the momentum increased and a series of policy measures and funding initiatives since then have succeeded in making widening participation a priority in all learning sectors (except perhaps the workplace). Many institutions have subsequently created dedicated managerial and other posts (or rebadged existing ones) with a specific widening participation brief and there has been a series of widening participation reports and good practice guides (see for example, CVCP, 1998; FEFC, 1997 and 2000 a and b; National Task Group for Widening Participation, 2000). There has also been a proliferation of campaigns, research projects, participation surveys and attitude surveys addressing the whole issue of participation and related themes such as barriers and motivation.

Widening participation in the current policy context

Engaging more people in learning is seen as a means of creating a culture of 'lifelong learning' – a key government objective the importance of which is underlined by the fact that a Lifelong Learning Directorate has been established and there have been four Ministers for Lifelong Learning since 1997.

For the Government, lifelong learning is closely linked with a range of other policy goals – economic advancement (the development of skills for the labour market); neighbourhood renewal; social inclusion and reduction of poverty; growth of active citizenship, and, rather further down in order of priority, overall cultural enrichment.

According to policy we need:

> *to build a new culture of learning and aspiration which will underpin national competitiveness and personal prosperity, encourage creativity and innovation and help build a more cohesive society.* (DfEE, 1999a)

This is a heavy and perhaps over-ambitious burden of responsibility to lay upon adult learning and it carries with it two related imperatives: that the people who do not currently engage in organised learning should be persuaded (or obliged) to do so for their own benefit as well as for that of the wider community and the national economy; and that education and training providers should make greater efforts to attract and cater for the groups who do not currently engage in organised learning.

Targets have been set to reduce the number of adults with poor literacy and numeracy; to raise the percentage of 16- to 18-year-olds in education; and to increase the number of students entering higher education. The Learning and Skills Council has also committed itself to setting targets to increase adult participation and the percentage of adults achieving at least a level 2 qualification.

Understandings of 'lifelong learning'

The shifts in educational terminology that have occurred over the last two or three decades have reflected successive policy changes. This is illustrated by some of the semantic changes that have taken place in higher education institutions:

> *The department through which the university has focused its activities has variously been called Extra-Mural, Adult and Continuing Education (DACE), Continuing Education (DCE), and, currently, the Centre for Lifelong Learning (CLL). These name changes are a reflection (although not always by design) of wider changes in respect of university provision for local adults.* (Whaley, 2000: 126)

> *What was once the Department of Extra-Mural Studies (serving the wider community) and then became the Centre for Continuing Education (offering accredited courses, access routes and professional development) is now the Office for Lifelong Learning (selling its wares to the paying public and increasingly involved in marketing institutional expertise).* (Martin, 2001)

One of the enduring characteristics of the adult learning field, however, is that the meaning and aims of whatever terminology and concepts are currently in vogue are always vigorously contested. Typically, therefore, opinions differ on what 'lifelong learning' actually means. Like many of the words used in discourses related to education, it is a notoriously elastic term that can be stretched or contracted to meet funding criteria or the policy need of the moment:

> *Lifelong learning appears in the literature and in political discourse in a bewildering number of different guises. For instance it is an instrument for change (in individuals, organisations and society) and as a buffer against change; a means of increasing competitiveness and of personal development; it is a social policy to combat social exclusion and to ease the re-entry of the unemployed into the labour market; it is a way of promoting the professional and social development of employees and of acquiring new knowledge through the labour process; it is a strategy to develop the participation of citizens in social, cultural and political affairs.* (Coffield, 1999:11–12)

In her timely critique, Jane Thompson (2001) observes that the term 'lifelong learning' permits so many things to be lumped together that it appears to have lost all meaning.

One reason why lifelong learning seems to be used with widespread approval is precisely because it glosses over other ways of thinking and speaking about education. Now competing interests and different agendas can shelter together under the same umbrella, providing an illusion of consensus. It allows for turf wars to be suspended and boundaries to be blurred (...) The secret of lifelong learning is that it means everything. But because it means everything, it is also in danger of meaning nothing. It is possible to attach it – like a kite-mark – to whatever initiative is seeking approval. Especially to initiatives that are seeking government funding. (Thompson, 2001: 8)

While declaring himself an 'unashamed advocate of lifelong learning', John Field also admits that the term has been devalued by the (paradoxical) tendency to use it as a convenient shorthand for post-compulsory education:

{it is} used by policy makers as little more than a modish repackaging of rather conventional policies for post-16 education and training, with little that is new or innovative. This tendency to wrap up existing practice in a more colourful phrase can also be seen in the rush by providers to claim their adherence to lifelong learning: annual reports, prospectuses, adult education brochures, and even professorial titles have all been subjected to this rebranding. The educational result is a kind of linguistic hyperinflation, in which the term in constantly devalued. (Field, 2000: viii-ix)

Three common approaches to lifelong learning have been summarised by Beverley Sand (1998). She uses S.J. Ball's (1990) categories of Modernisers, Progressives and Cultural Restorationists to identify 'the different and often conflicting elements which appear in debates about the concept.'

According to Sand, the position of the Modernisers is characterised by an emphasis on economic relevance and relationship to the market, that of the Progressives by an emphasis on social justice, democracy and responsiveness to the community, while the Cultural Restorationists' position is characterised by a concern for the preservation of traditional values and academic standards.

Among the Modernisers she places those concerned with low skill levels who interpret lifelong learning as a means of increasing employability and improving national competitiveness; among the Progressives she includes those concerned with radical or 'social purpose' adult education, and among the Cultural Restorationists she includes those concerned to maintain existing institutional traditions, practices and standards. She argues that while these three different views of lifelong learning co-exist and are given equal weight in many reports and documents, the one that chimes most with government thinking and priorities will determine the direction of policy:

A range of different and contradictory meanings has emerged in relation to the concept of lifelong learning, often within the same reports and papers and frequently between groups and individuals who believe they are discussing the same thing. Radical and Progressive ideas about the transformation of society and the place of individuals within it, along with Cultural Restorationist views of lifelong learning in an ordered society, are able to sit, if a little uneasily, alongside the Modernist view of a learning market, with learners as elective consumers, enthusiastically engaging in lifelong learning as necessary to update their skills and knowledge throughout their lives in response to the economic imperatives of the nation. While each of these positions may have equal value in terms of the lifelong learning debate and make an equal contribution to the matrix of meanings, it is their relative influence on government policy and practice which will have the most effect in determining which of these positions will dominate the implementation of any lifelong learning agenda. (Sand, 1998: 25)

As will be argued in later chapters, it appears to be the Modernisers and Restorationists who currently have the upper hand and this is helping to shape the forms that widening participation strategies are currently taking as well as some of the assumptions underlying them. The particular influence of the first group also explains the vein of coercion that some feel runs through current lifelong learning policies. Field (2000), for example, points out how much current learning is in fact not voluntary but obligatory: 'for a growing number of people, for lengthening periods of their lives (...) particularly (...) for those who are in paid employment or who are unemployed and in receipt of benefit' p119), while Coffield believes this trend has already taken a sinister direction:

(...) a sceptical version of lifelong learning (...) has received little attention in the country. Namely, that it has become a form of social control and has the potential to become so ever more powerfully. (Coffield, 1999: 12)

Nevertheless the term 'lifelong learning' has a useful blandness that disavows such reservations. It manages to convey the suggestion that it is an essentially desirable process against which no-one could possibly argue, as some of the people interviewed for this study have found:

Lifelong learning is seen as fundamentally desirable to the point where there is some political correctness about the term.

The slogans of lifelong learning and the underlying values they're meant to express are unexplored. But if you raise questions about it, it looks as though you're against the whole idea.

The term's lack of a universally-accepted definition is also politically useful:

When people suggest that the notion of lifelong learning is meaningless because it cannot be defined (...) they are right insofar as its ambivalence defies attempts to locate it within the powerful boundaries of definition. They are wrong insofar as they miss the point that lifelong learning is an ambivalent space traversed by many different practices; it is both about nothing and everything, capable of being inscribed and enacted in many different forms. (Edwards, 2000: 32-33)

Understandings of widening participation

The various meanings attached to lifelong learning are reflected in the kinds of approaches and strategies that providers are being encouraged (or choose) to adopt to widen participation. And, like 'lifelong learning', 'widening participation' is understood differently by different people. Definitions of the term vary according to the professional position and political perspectives of those who use it, as well as to the specific institutional or funding context. Some feel that this has diminished the specificity and usefulness of the term:

Within institutions, the different political perspectives of different practitioners contest similar terminology. Resources are allocated within the criteria of current policy but the definitions of those policies continue to be debated by funders, managers and practitioners. Consequently, projects to engage a broader section of our communities in learning are often based on competing philosophical beliefs that have different implications and effects for those 'participating' (...) It is important to be specific about the claims made of the activity. Otherwise widening participation in education is in danger of being all things to all people and pleasing none of them. (Stuart, 2000: 23).

In policy documents, non-participation in organised learning tends to be viewed largely as a problem, with the people concerned described negatively as non-learners with learning deficits, especially poor basic skills, that exclude them from the mainstream of society and lead them into such undesirable situations as unemployment, dependency on the state, run-down living conditions and crime. In policy, therefore, widening participation in learning has important social as well as economic aims and is a process that is intended to change the behaviour and hence the prospects of the socially excluded and 'disaffected'. The implication is that those who do not engage in learning should do so in the interests of enhancing their chances in a shifting labour market. This would help to reduce poverty and exclusion and make a contribution to the local and national economy. Irrespective of the soundness of these respective assumptions, this enjoins on people, especially those classified as 'non-learners', a certain sense of moral responsibility to engage in purposeful learning.

Education providers see widening participation largely as a process or set of processes which aim to redress imbalances in the kind of people they attract. Depending on who you speak to, the term is also applied loosely to types of provision (for example, basic skills) or to particular client groups under-represented in mainstream provision.

The Kennedy report *Learning Works* (1997) defined widening participation as a broad and inclusive process incorporating stages such as access, achievement and progression for groups often under-represented in further education. The FEFC (1997) guide to good practice also employed this definition:

> *bringing more students from under-represented and disadvantaged groups into education and training; ensuring that these students stay on their programmes; extending the ways through which they can learn and achieve; and ensuring that they progress to suitable* [sic] *destinations.*

Some providers, however, define the term more narrowly and view widening participation principally as an access process designed to make the student cohort more ethnically and geographically representative of the communities served. This can variously entail recruitment strategies, outreach development work in local communities, delivery of guidance and provision in local venues, collaboration and partnerships with other agencies and more flexible entry criteria. Most of these strategies are concentrated outside the institution and do not involve any substantial changes to mainstream practices, established procedures or the curriculum. As I found over a decade ago (McGivney, 1990), institutional widening participation measures tend primarily to involve the pre-entry and entry stages. It is far more common for newly-recruited learners to be expected to adapt to the practices of a learning institution than for institutions to adapt their practices to a changing body of learners (although the notion of inclusive learning proposed in the Tomlinson Report (FEFC, 1996) has stimulated a welcome move in this direction in further education).

The limitations of this approach have been the subject of some debate, especially in higher education institutions where many of the staff engaged in processes and projects to improve access believe that widening participation should involve an adjustment of mainstream procedures and practices, including the curriculum:

> *Are we talking about extending access to the same old (excluding) curricula and systems? Offering a marginal (inferior) kind of provision? Creating opportunities in (not quite education but) training? Opening up different bits of the HE system to different kinds of students (university of excellence/university of inclusion)? Or do we mean participation in relevant, inclusive, challenging, transformative learning experiences? What is the nature of the participation? What is the education in which we want to encourage and effect?* (Whaley, 2000: 125).

Among providers and teaching staff there are, then, two radically different views of what the term widening participation means: one is about 'enabling greater access to unchanging patterns of provision' (Bamber *et al*, 2000: 159); the other is about tailoring learning to the needs, priorities and preferences of the groups who are excluded. Between these polar understandings of the term, it is possible to find the term used in a variety of ways. In recent years it has come increasingly to mean provision of learning activities of a remedial nature and, by extension, 'widening participation' students are understood to be those with poor literacy skills, and low qualification levels:

> *I would define widening participation students as those who left school with poor levels of skills and no qualifications who haven't made any attempt since leaving school to rectify this and don't see it as a deficiency, but who may come forward for other instrumental reasons such as to help their kids.* (Intervewee)

Like 'lifelong learning', 'widening participation' implies something that is essentially desirable which therefore should be universally acceptable, although some have questioned whether participation in learning is always 'a good thing' (Schuller, 2000). Both have become catch-all phrases that can be interpreted in a variety of ways and which can camouflage as much as they reveal. This is a feature of much of the language used in European social and educational policy. For example, (Field 2000: 108) notes the increasing tendency during the 1990s to replace words such as poverty or inequality with broader, less explicit terms such as 'social exclusion'. Others have noted the widespread use of the word 'learning' to replace 'education and training'.

Understandings of 'learning'

The current policy preoccupation with 'increasing demand for learning' begs the question: what *kind* of learning? In policy documents, learning is more often seen as a process of acquiring knowledge, skills and competences for the labour market than as a process leading to deeper understanding, personal enrichment and development and wider social and democratic outcomes.

Moreover, as Atkin (2000) has pointed out, despite the semantic variations on the theme of learning in recent years – the 'learning society'; 'lifelong' or 'lifetime learning'; the 'learning culture'; and the 'learning age' – it is formal education that remains the reality (i.e. the priority). In policy documents, learning is invariably defined as an engagement in organised education provision and when fundamental or 'step' changes in participation are called for, it is invariably increased participation in formal education provision that is intended. As argued in Chapter 2, this view separates people into participants and non-participants, and reinforces the tendency to attribute non-participation largely to the negative attitudes and lack of motivation of individuals.

There is, however, another view of participation which understands learning as a social activity embedded in a social context. This approach sees learning as a process involving all kinds and forms of learning; it sees all people as learners, and considers all types of learning to have validity. This view accepts that people learn from experience and from diverse types of activity within all the different dimensions of their lives – family life, social life, working life and community life.

These two concepts of learning are currently separate and unconnected. However, it may only be possible to create a real culture of lifelong learning if all the different types of learning in which people engage are recognised, valued and brought together in a dynamic and mutually-reinforcing relationship. This means recognising and valuing the different types of learning that people achieve to a greater or lesser degree throughout their life-span.

This does not mean that inconsistent and uneven access to structured learning opportunities is not important and does not need to be addressed. I make no apology for repeating what I said in *Education's for Other People*: unequal participation in organised learning opportunities is an indictment 'not of public apathy but of an education system which still projects a narrow and elitist image.' (McGivney, 1990: 175-176).

Some question, however, whether we actually should try to widen participation given that for some people learning may be associated with 'coercion, boredom and repeated failure' (Field, 2000: 118). Field also argues that learning is already compulsory for a growing number of people – for those in work because of factors such as regulatory frameworks, statutory requirements, contract compliance and customer or client expectations; and for the unemployed because of Benefit and New Deal requirements. More recently, creeping compulsion has been catching up with those in receipt of benefits who have poor basic skills. This, according to Field, obliges us to reconsider traditional views of participation:

> *Conventionally, non-participants have always been seen by Adult Education writers as victims of social structures or psychological defects denied equal access to a positive opportunity. Participants on the other hand are regarded as willing volunteers (...) As lifelong learning becomes generalised and adult participation ceases to be largely voluntary in nature, these accepted wisdoms must be challenged.* (Field, 2000: 120-121)

What is meant by 'participation' is, of course, the subject of continuing debate. Some even question whether it is a meaningful concept, given the diversity of adult learning (see Edwards, 1997). However, so long as we still have a post-compulsory sector receiving a significant amount of public funds we should be concerned to see that it is accessible to and used by the whole adult population, rather than an active minority. The following chapters will consider the extent to which this has been achieved since 1990 and whether it is actually achievable.

Chapter 2

Identifying the pattern

Increase or decline in participation?

Since the end of the 1980s, there has been an increasing drive by both the current and the previous governments to measure the amount of adult learning that takes place. This has been partly in response to the establishment of national education and training targets agreed in 1991 and revised in 1995. However, it has always proved difficult to determine the exact rate of overall adult participation in organised learning as it depends on the age cohorts surveyed and the various definitions of learning used, differences in which lead to considerable variations in findings:

> There is no single accepted definition of an 'adult learner' in the literature – either in terms of who is an adult, or what constitutes learning. The different definitions are reflected in the various sources of statistical data and, to an extent, in the results that they portray, ie the wider the definition of learning, the greater the apparent number of participants. (Hillage and Aston, 2001: 5)

According to the Labour Force Survey (LFS) which covers adults of working age and asks about the education and training undertaken in the four weeks prior to the survey, about 13 per cent of adults were participating in learning activity at the end of 1998, excluding those attending full-time education. As the survey only covers a four-week period and excludes 'leisure classes' (a notoriously imprecise term) this figure must be a significant under-estimate of the actual number of adults engaged in organised learning activities at the time.

Regular surveys of adults aged 17 and above have been undertaken by NIACE (the national organisation for adult learning) since 1991. These have employed a wider definition of learning:

Learning could mean practising, studying, or reading about something. It can also mean being taught, instructed or coached. This is so you can develop skills, knowledge, abilities or understanding of something. Learning can also be called education or training. You can do it regularly (each day or month) or you can do it for a short period of time. It can be full-time or part-time, done at home, at work, or in another place like a college. Learning does not have to lead to a qualification. We are interested in any learning you have done, whether or not it was finished.

The NIACE survey in 1996 found that 23 per cent of respondents were currently learning and that 40-41 per cent were either in full-time education or had undertaken some other form of learning in the previous three years or since leaving full-time education (Sargant *et al*, 1997). In subsequent surveys conducted in 1999 and 2000 there was little change: 22 per cent of those surveyed reported that they were currently studying and 40-41 per cent that they had been learning in the previous three years (Tuckett and Sargant, 1999; *Adults Learning*, 2000). In her Introduction to *The Learning Divide Revisited* Naomi Sargant (2000: iii) observed that 'despite the range of measures taken to expand publicly funded learning, participation overall remains static'. The NIACE 2001 survey, however, has revealed a significant increase in participation: 29 per cent of participants said they were currently learning and 46 per cent that they were current learners or had engaged in learning over the last three years (see Table 1). One of the biggest increases appears to have been among part-time workers.

Table 1	**Participation Trends 1996-2001**				
		1996	**1999**	**2000**	**2001**
	Base – all respondents = 100%	4,673	5,054	4,091	6,310
Total	Current	23	22	22	29
	Recent	17	18	19	17
	Current/Recent	40	40	41	46
	None since full-time education	36	37	36	33
Men	Current	25	24	24	32
	Recent	18	18	19	17
	Current/Recent	43	41	43	49
	None since full-time education	31	34	33	29
Women	Current	21	21	21	27
	Recent	17	19	18	17
	Current/Recent	38	40	39	44
	None since full-time education	41	40	39	37

Source: Aldridge and Tuckett, 2001

Taken as a whole, the NIACE surveys suggest that adult participation has risen since the late 1980s (the national surveys cited in *Education's for Other People* (McGivney, 1990) suggested 10-15 per cent of adults were participating at any given time). Unlike those summarised in *Education's for Other People*, however, the NIACE surveys include people in full-time education, which accounts for some of the increase. Even so, the levels of adult participation indicated by the NIACE surveys are significantly lower than those revealed by the National Adult Learning Survey (NALS) which was conducted among adults aged 16–69 in 1997 (Beinart and Smith, 1998). This found that, excluding those still in full-time continuing education, 67 per cent of respondents had undertaken some taught or non-taught vocational learning and 30 per cent some non-vocational learning in the previous three years, while 23 per cent had done both. NALS' definition of learning included both taught and non-taught learning, defined as follows:

Taught learning could be: any courses that were meant to lead to qualifications; any taught courses designed to help you develop skills that you might use in a job; any courses, instruction or tuition in driving, in playing a musical instrument, in an art or craft, in a sport or in any practical skill; evening classes; learning which has involved working on your own from a package of materials; any other taught course, instruction or tuition.

Non-taught learning might be: studying for qualifications without taking part in a taught course; supervised training while you were actually doing a job; time spent keeping up to date with developments in the type of work you do without taking part in a taught course; deliberately trying to improve your knowledge about anything or teach yourself a skill without taking part in a taught course.

Some feel that this definition accounts for the higher rate of reported participation (see Tight, 1998).[1] However, the real reason may be that NALS involved longer interviews than the NIACE surveys, which allowed people time to recall their learning in more detail.

As suggested above, the increase in the numbers of adults engaging in organised learning could be explained by higher staying-on rates. Citing evidence from a household survey in Wales, Gorard (2000a: 5) argues that apparent progress towards lifelong learning targets may be due to:

passing young people with extended initial education into the category of 'working-age' and passing older people with few episodes of participation or qualification out of it. (...) Once this is taken into account the impact of the {lifelong learning} policy is non-

---

1 Detailed comparisons between national survey findings can be found in Smith and Spurling (1999) and Hillage *et al* (2000).

existent. In fact, despite the calls for lifelong learning, adults may be now less likely to take part in learning as adults than they were 20 or even 50 years ago.

Field (2001a: 25) also questions the conclusion that overall adult engagement in learning has increased. His analysis of LFS data shows that the share of all learning taken by people over 25 has fallen 'steadily and dramatically' over the last five years while the share of learning among those aged 16–24 has risen. When he compared LFS data for the years between 1995 and 2000, it could be seen that whereas there was a substantial concentration of job-related learning among people in their late teens and those aged 20-24, the share of learing in later years of working life had steadily declined.

Field also cites General Household Study data showing that between 1993 and 1996 the proportion of people taking non-accredited leisure courses in adult education classes provided by local authorities fell sharply while those attending FE courses increased. He concluded:

> *Among adults, participation in organised learnng is certainly changing, but neither survey provides clear evidence that it is growing in its importance. Quite possibly it is not growing at all, but declining relative to the steady extension of learning among teenagers. Through the 1990s, work-related learning became more concentrated among young people and recent policy initiatives such as Education Maintenance Allowances will ensure that initial education is extended further.* (Field, 2001a: 26)

Similarly, Field (2001a) attributes the increase in learning among part-time workers revealed in the NIACE 2001 survey to the increase in full-time (younger) students obliged to seek part-time work to support themselves. Thus this development could be more a by-product of central funding policies than a result of widening participation strategies.

The composition of adult learners

Irrespective of the actual numbers participating, there have been some significant changes in adult participation patterns over the last decade. Since 1990, the further and higher education sectors have expanded and the student body has become more diverse with a significant growth in the number of mature and part-time students, women students and students from minority ethnic communities. According to the Further Education Funding Council (FEFC) (2000), about two thirds of the 3.5 million students studying further education courses in colleges in 1997/98 were aged 25 and over, although this growth subsequently tailed off (Robinson, 2000).

Most were studying part-time in general further education or tertiary colleges for lower level qualifications.

In the same year, adults formed the majority of students in higher education and just under 37 per cent of first year degree entrants were 25 and over (Hillage *et al*, 2000). In 2001, students over 25 accounted for 45 per cent of the total student body compared with 35 per cent ten years before (Warwick, 2001).

Another significant change has been the number of women entering further and higher education. In November 1999, 59 per cent of those enrolled on FEFC-funded courses were women (*FEFC Council News*, 2000) and the number of women students in higher education has now reached parity with men.

What all the surveys show, however, is that, as a whole, participants in organised learning are no more representative of the whole population than they were 10 years ago. There has been growth in participation but less 'breadth'. As Uden (1996) has memorably pointed out, participation can increase without it being 'meaningfully' widened. More recently, Hillage *et al* (2000) have reminded us that many groups and individuals remain excluded from education and training, most specifically those in the lower income, lower socio-economic groups.

Despite their different findings regarding the numbers of adults engaged in learning, the NALS and NIACE surveys show, like all their predecessors, that those who typically engage in organised forms of learning are younger adults, those who continued their education after the age of 16 and acquired qualifications and those in paid employment.

The surveys also indicate that there are significant disparities in participation between different regions which, it has been suggested, could reflect the composition of local populations and local labour market conditions (Hillage *et al*, 2000).

Certain trends seem stubbornly resistant to change: the decrease in participation with age, the link between school leaving age and later participation and the link between participation and occupational status. All surveys indicate that those who are employed are far more likely to participate in education or training than those who are unemployed or economically inactive. NALS (1997), for example, revealed stark differences between employed and unemployed respondents with a large majority of the former and less than half of the latter reporting learning activity in the previous three years. A more recent survey from the Nestlé Family Monitor (2001) found that the majority of learners were employed whereas only 26per cent of unemployed respondents had undertaken learning activities in the previous 12 months. However, employed participants are far more likely to have worked in managerial, professional or associate professional occupations than in manual occupations.

As in the past, therefore, the strongest difference between those who describe themselves as learners and those who do not is still social class and the increase in the overall numbers of people participating has been largely among those in the higher socio-economic groups. In the NIACE 1999 and 2000 surveys, for example, over half of respondents in socio-economic group AB (professional, managerial) were current or recent learners compared with just over a third of respondents in group C2 (skilled working class) and about a quarter of those in DE (unskilled and on limited incomes). The NIACE 1999 survey also suggested that the increase in participation among AB respondents had been accompanied by an actual decline in participation among DE respondents. The most recent NIACE survey (2001) shows that although participation has risen within all social groups, the sharpest increase has again been among those in categories AB and C1. Among those in the professional and managerial category, there has been a 20 per cent increase in participation since 1996. As the commentary on the findings suggests:

There is nothing to be complacent about. The distribution of the expansion in opportunity is heavily weighted to the educationally privileged, to the young and to people with jobs. (Aldridge and Tuckett, 2001: 5)

Table 2	**Trends in current/recent learning by social class**				
	% change	1996	1999	2000	2001
Total sample	(+6)	40	40	41	46
AB	(+14)	53	58	60	67
C1	(+7)	52	51	52	59
C2	(+8)	33	36	35	41
DE	(+2)	26	24	26	28
Source: Aldridge and Tuckett, 2001					

Wide social class differentials were also revealed by NALS (1997) within its higher overall statistical picture of participation.

Such findings have prompted the conclusion that class is still the key to understanding the 'learning divide' (Sargant, 2000). Longitudinal research studies have produced evidence to substantiate this view. Studies of a cohort born in 1958 show that, while there has been a general improvement in girls' prospects, social class still has a major impact on people's life chances. The data suggest that children from working-class backgrounds and born into poverty are no more likely to obtain qualifications than they were several decades ago, no matter how bright they are (Bynner *et al*, 2000). Nevertheless this should be seen in the context of the significant progress we have made towards greater educational equality since 1944.

Progress in the twentieth century has led to considerable improvements in social inclusion and opportunities by gender, ethnicity, and class, and these improvements apply to education as much as any other social phenomenon. It would be inappropriate to deny, or downplay, this progress. Whatever our complaints may be in retrospect, the 1944 Education Act, the comprehensivisation of schools, perhaps even the 1988 Education Reform Act and a host of other initiatives, have all attempted to produce greater social justice in our education system, and to some extent they have all succeeded. (Gorard, 2000a: 1-2)

Although surveys can, at best, yield only a crude and superficial snapshot of adult learning behaviour, and the standard socio-economic classifications used are widely considered inadequate, the general consistency of research and survey findings confirms that there are still stark imbalances in participation in organised forms of learning, with those who are poorest and most socially disadvantaged participating least. This is compounded by a relatively new factor – the 'information divide' between adults with access to the new technologies and those without access:

Access to new communications technologies is heavily slanted to upper socio-economic groups, to the younger age groups and to those with access through the workplace or an educational or other organisation (...) The danger is that the emerging information divide will reinforce the learning divide and that the two deficits will feed on each other (Sargant, 2000: xi).

In the NIACE 1999 survey, 43 per cent of respondents with access to the internet said they were currently learning, compared with 18 per cent of those without internet access. Those with internet access were also twice as likely to say that they would take up learning in the future as people without access. The NIACE 2001 survey also suggests that there is a strong correlation between access to the internet and current learning and intentions to learn.

Participation in higher education

The imbalances in participation revealed by successive surveys and enquiries have fuelled the policy emphasis on widening participation. Most recently this has focused on higher education where 'class remains the stubborn barrier to distribution by merit' (Halsey, 1998) despite the development of new and more flexible entry routes.

The Dearing report into higher education (NCIHE, 1997) expressed concerns about the continuing paucity of entrants from the lowest social categories – a situation that had remained virtually unchanged since the Robbins Report in the 1960s (Great Britain Committee on Higher Education, 1963). While there has been a marked increase in the numbers of mature students, their social class profile roughly approximates that of younger students. Although special access measures, changes in learning modes and delivery of higher education provision in further education have been major factors in increased participation in the last decade, they have done little to alter the social composition of the student body. Data from the Universities and Colleges Admissions Service (UCAS) shows little shift in the social class profile of those admitted to universities. In 1994 only 17 per cent of home applicants accepted on degree courses came from an unskilled occupational background and this figure was virtually unchanged in 1998 (Tonks, 1999). In 1999 the three highest socio-economic groups accounted for 64 per cent of undergraduates while those from the lowest three accounted for 24 per cent. Thus, although the age and gender composition of higher education students has changed, people from the lower income groups still face difficulties in gaining access (Goddard, 2000a; Bamber and Tett, 2001). While there has been some improvement in their participation rates, 'these have not succeeded in narrowing the gap in participation between those from the most and the least affluent groups'. (Woodrow, 2000a:15)

This situation is viewed with concern among some sections of the academic community. Woodrow (2001) argues that social class presents the biggest obstacle to wider participation in higher education. It is a major factor which interacts with gender, ethnicity, age and disability in maintaining the overall elitism of the sector and the continuing under-representation of lower income and working class people – a view underlined by Robertson's (1997b) memorable claim that a person from Richmond in Surrey is 250 times more likely to go to university than a person in Everton, a district in Liverpool. In fact, 'A student from Richmond-on-Thames is more likely to find a place in one of the Liverpool universities than a local citizen born and educated a few hundred yards away.' (Robertson, 1997b: 13-14)

Moreover, the people who enter the sector via non-traditional (non-A-Level) routes are differentiated from the conventional student body in several ways. Access applicants tend to be mature, from the lower social groups, and often of Black or Asian ethnic origin, whereas applicants accepted with A level qualifications tend to be under 21 years old, white and from the three higher social groups. (Davidson-Burnett and Green, 1999)

The distribution of 'non-traditional' students has also been uneven across the sector as a whole. They are largely to be found in a small number of institutions, especially the newer universities and the Open University, rather than being distributed evenly throughout the sector (Robertson, 1997b; Preece, 1998, Field, 2000). Sixty-five per cent of all ethnic minority students, for example, enter the system via the new universities (Robertson, 1997b). A similar situation obtains in Scotland where it is almost entirely the 'new' universities that have admitted a more diverse student body. (Bamber *et al*, 2000)

Research also indicates that there is a hierarchy of higher education subject areas related to age, gender, social class, ethnicity and qualifications held on entry (Davidson-Burnett and Green, 1999). Thus Field (2000: 42) refers to 'sizeable disparities' between institutions, with the largest numbers of adults usually found in the least prestigious universities, and between subjects, with adults confined largely to the social sciences and humanities.

In brief:

> *The participation gap between the most affluent and the least affluent groups exists at all age levels; for all modes of learning; is widest in the most prestigious HEIs and in subjects most in demand; has persisted despite 30 years of widening participation strategies.* (Woodrow, 2000b)

The excluded sections of the community

The evidence overall, therefore, indicates that adult participation is 'lop-sided' (Forrester and Payne, 2000) and that many segments of the population are still glaringly under-represented in adult, further and higher education. These include the following (now familiar) large groupings:

- *Disaffected school leavers and those with poor school experiences.*
- *Those on low incomes or receiving benefits, and living in particular deprived postcode areas.*
- *Those in difficult living circumstances (e.g. the homeless; young people leaving care).*
- *People who are out of or on the fringes of the labour market* (the unemployed, the unwaged, the retired, those with health and disability problems).
- *Older adults*: the participation of adults over 60 dropped after 1992 and continues to decrease. The NIACE 1999 survey found a 20 per cent reduction in participation by retired people over the previous three years (Tuckett and Sargant, 1999).
- *Unskilled manual workers, part-time employees and workers in small and medium sized enterprises*: according to Bryan Sanderson, Chair of the Learning and Skills Council, almost a third of British workers receive no formal training from their employers (Crequer, 2000).
- *Some groups of ethnic minorities* including Afro-Caribbean men; some groups of Asian women; travellers, asylum seekers and refugees.
- *People with learning difficulties*: according to the findings of a NIACE project on the impact of the Further and Higher Education Act (summarised in Joseph Rowntree Foundation, 1996) participation among adults with learning difficulties increased after 1992. However, while provision increased for people with moderate learning difficulties, it lessened for those with severe or profound/complex learning difficulties. A later NIACE survey (Joseph Rowntree

Foundation, 1998) found that although there were some appropriate and imaginative classes for adults with learning difficulties, overall provision was scanty with classes often fragile and vulnerable to cuts.
- *People with disabilities*: this group is still severely under-represented in all forms of provision. Robertson (1997:18-19) reported that, in 1997, higher education students who reported a disability represented approximately 2 per cent of the total student body.
- *Offenders and ex-offenders*: Reports suggest that there has been a narrowing of education opportunities for this group. (Sanders, 2000)

The wider picture

Many of these groups (with the exception of older adults) have been prioritised in measures introduced to widen participation. However, by identifying some groups it is easy to miss others and lose some of the complexities of adult participation. Gorard (2000a) argues that if extended initial education and improved qualification rates among young people are not taken into account, a more accurate picture of exclusion emerges. In south Wales, for example, surveys have indicated that women as well as older adults are among the excluded groups. In other words, the fact that overall participation is growing may be intensifying the exclusion of some groups:

> *Participation and qualifications are improving, while the differences between sectors and social groups are declining. These changes mean that the same indicators are also moving slowly in the same direction for the adult population, as people leave initial education for the workforce. However, once these 'conveyor belt' changes are separated out, there is no progress in participation and qualifications for adults while they are adults, and the differentials between some sectors and social groups are increasing over time.* (Gorard, 2000a: 6)

Field (2000) also believes that progress in extending initial education and increases in adult participation may be creating an underclass among those left behind. He refers to official concern on this subject expressed by the Select Committee on Education and Employment (1999) and to a report (DfEE 2000a) which remarked on 'a worrying trend for the skills-rich to extend their learning and competence while the skills-poor fall further behind'.

Similar fears were expressed by several of the people interviewed during the course of this study:

There are more opportunities for people to gain education at school so there's a different client group now. Those left behind are the really deprived. People are just as oppressed now. The gaps between people are wider than they've ever been. (Interviewee)

Theoretically, the rise in initial qualification levels should lead to an increase in adult participation, and numerically, the numbers of participants in organised education and training seem to be rising. But the learning divide between different areas and social classes remains and is getting deeper as the gap widens between those who gain qualifications and those who are left behind. We should be optimistic. In schools there's been progress in exam results which means that another generation will be coming through with qualifications and that should lead to greater participation so we should see some difference. But in reality there's a learning divide that's getting deeper and deeper. Surveys show that the proportion of people who are employed with the same employer hasn't changed but the biggest changes are with the unskilled. There are many more people unoccupied now in our big cities. For example, unemployment figures in Sheffield are double the differential between the best and worst areas in the last 5 or 6 years. This is a polarisation that cuts right across widening participation and shows how incredibly difficult it is to make progress. (Interviewee)

Some of the positive changes that have taken place in adult participation over the last decade camouflage some continuing differences and inequities. For example, although women are now well represented numerically in further and higher education, the NIACE and NALS surveys suggest that, at any given time, more men than women engage in learning. (This is despite data from the annual Labour Force Surveys which suggest that a slightly higher proportion of women participate in training than men – a situation that is often attributed to the growing numbers of women entering or returning to the labour force and receiving induction and basic training). There are also clear differences in men's and women's participation patterns. Men engage in learning mainly for instrumental purposes and participate in fewer sectors than women. Women use a wider range of educational routes and are concerned not only with work-related learning but also with self-development and wider societal and community participation. They also follow more flexible qualification routes than men. There are also very clear differences in the subjects studied (McGivney, 1998a). Hence Field (2000) argues that the near-equality in numbers revealed by aggregate data conceals continuing gender imbalances in participation. For, while their overall numbers have increased, women students are still significantly under-represented in some subject and discipline areas and the participation of working-class women in any form of organised learning has remained low. Robertson (1997b: 16) also makes the point that whereas more women are entering university than ever before, this does not mean they have reached a position of equality: they are still disadvantaged by factors such as the type of institutions they enter, the subjects they study, the age at which they gain qualifications and their labour market position after graduation. He quotes Blackburn and Jarman (1993):

> *The present situation is still one of considerable inequality which helps to maintain the inequalities which run through the whole of our society (...) It would be wrong to assume that the progress means that women have stopped suffering discrimination (...) In one sense there has been a tendency to reinforce inequalities in that the number of women entering higher education has increased more in the lower status – especially part-time – courses than in full-time university courses.* (p210)

As Steele (2000) argues, the elite universities, courses and most prestigious qualifications are still largely the preserve of white men from more affluent backgrounds.

Like women, minority ethnic communities are now well represented in post-16 education. A significantly higher proportion of individuals from minority ethnic groups stay on in full-time education than members of the white population, and FEFC statistics show that communities of black African, Indian, Pakistani, Bangladeshi and Chinese origin are over-represented in FEFC-funded provision in relation to their proportion in the overall population (although Bangladeshi and Pakistani women as well as Afro-Caribbean men are significantly under-represented). In higher education, however, their situation is similar to that of women. Robertson (1997b) quotes studies showing that, although they are no longer under-represented as a whole, there are significant differences between groups and inequalities relating to the institutions entered and modes of study – an analysis confirmed by the Commission on the Future of Multi-Ethnic Britain launched in October 2000 (Goddard, 2000b). Similarly, Haque (2001) reports that a study of an inner city university showed marked gender disparities within minority ethnic groups as well as *'a greater proportion of students from higher social classes even within the ethnic minority communities'.* (p11)

Viewed as a whole, these findings suggest that although there were some positive changes in the age, gender and ethnic composition of adult learners during the last decade, we have still failed to bring about real equality and a better social balance in organised forms of learning. In fact participation among some groups has actually decreased in the last decade. These include the lowest socio-economic groups, the elderly, and people in areas hit by industrial decline such as South Wales where a long-term study has revealed a significant drop in participation in adult learning associated with the decline of the coal-mining industry and the accompanying collapse of trade unionism and political engagement:

> *Despite the improvement in terms of numerical participation in Wales since 1996, it remains true that almost a third of the population (34 per cent) reported no episodes of*

learning since full-time continuous education. A larger recent survey of industrial South Wales confirms this, but actually suggests an even gloomier picture. One third of the respondents there reported no formal education or training since compulsory school leaving age and in several cases even before that age. (Gorard 2000b: 187)

There also seems to have been little movement in achievement levels. DfEE annual reports on progress towards national learning targets show improvement among people under 18 but very 'limited progress amongst those older than statutory school age' (*Working Brief*, 2000). FEFC (2000a) has found that learners from the groups least likely to participate are also those with lower retention and achievement rates.

This situation, combined with persistent reports of the high incidence of poor basic skills among British adults, has prompted a veritable barrage of policy measures aiming to coax or coerce people back into organised learning to increase their skills and qualification levels. A failure to engage in learning is commonly attributed to the apathy and negative attitudes of those concerned:

(...) *a disturbing number of adults appear to be disinterested in further learning or cannot see its relevance to them. If we are to achieve the step increase in skills amongst adults which we need, we must find ways of reaching this group, changing their attitudes and overcoming their inertia. This will require more than simple advocacy or promotion of learning, it will require convincing adults, individually in the most extreme cases, of the real benefits of learning.* (DfEE 2000a)

As was suggested in Chapter 1, however, we need to consider what is meant by 'learning'.

Informal learning

Forrester and Payne (2000) question whether a definition of participation which only takes into account formal learning and which adopts a snapshot approach to participation at a particular point in time can encapsulate the complexity of adult learning patterns. A study of community views of adult education and training (Bowman *et al*, 2000: 7-8) has also concluded that the classification of people in opposing groups such as participants and non-participants, learners and non-learners, achievers and low achievers, enthusiastic or reluctant learners, is an over-simplification. It reflects neither the role of education and training in people's lives, nor the ways in which the relationships between education, training and work are perceived or experienced. Moreover, such definitions depend largely on how people self-report, and it is often found that respondents to surveys do not necessarily share the definitions of learning used. Even when presented with broad definitions of learning, people do not always report less formal learning episodes even if these take the form of structured courses. Bowman *et al*'s study found that some people who said that they were not currently engaged in any form of education and training were in fact attending non-accredited courses at a local community centre or engaged in learning activities in organisations in which the main remit or orientation was not education.

It is often found that people do not mention participation in 'leisure' courses or informal learning activities in survey responses because they do not regard these as involving 'proper' or 'serious' learning. This is hardly surprising, given the strongly instrumental emphasis of policy in recent years:

> *The emphasis, particularly for funding purposes, on vocational and qualification-based courses, is likely to have affected people's definitions of what learning constitutes. The increasing use of the term 'leisure' courses, while not necessarily meant to be derogatory, does imply that they are of less value than vocational ones, at least in the sense that they are not legitimated for funding purposes.* (Sargant *et al*, 1997: 32)

> *Estimates of participation levels depend heavily on the definition of 'learning' that is used. Formal episodes of learning such as degree courses, attendance at training colleges, formal training courses organised by the employer at work and so on tend to be immediately identified by survey respondents as learning activities, but they are less clear about including informal, unstructured types of learning. This is particularly true of some learning at work that is seen as 'just part of the job'. It is also true of some types of non-vocational learning because the purpose of the activity is seen as fun rather than learning. This raises the fundamental question of what constitutes learning and whether it can be clearly differentiated from such things as experience and leisure.* (Edwards *et al*, 1998)

Conversely, when people do report less formal learning episodes, these are not always recorded:

> *Studies in Wales may be over-emphasising the importance of formal participation and certified episodes as opposed to more personal experiences of substantive learning. Non-participants often report important periods of substantive but informal learning, which is nevertheless downplayed in official reports, and therefore the research based on it, since it does not contribute to the impact of National Training Targets.* (Gorard, 2000b)

As this suggests, what is referred to as 'learning' in official documents is often a relatively narrow and restricted notion. Although NALS (1997) and its successor the *Participation in Adult Learning Survey* (PALS) (Lavalle and Finch, 1999) tried to capture the broader types of learning in which people engage by including a wider range of questions, the categories of learning used (self-directed learning, independent study for qualifications, supervised on-the-job training, skills up-dating and improvement of knowledge) are still largely skewed towards conventional perceptions of learning. The definitions of learning employed in surveys cannot be too inclusive but currently they leave out a vast amount of learning that occurs as part of people's social, cultural and leisure activities.

Research studies have found that people from working-class and low income groups – in other words, those usually identified as non-participants in surveys – are frequently learning as part of their involvement in activities connected to their everyday lives. In areas where participation in formal learning is ostensibly low, for example, it is possible to find many adults engaged in a rich diversity of learning activities that are related to their personal interests and community needs (McGivney, 1999a). For example, several studies have demonstrated that community activism and engagement in social movements such as environmental protection (Brookfield, 1986; Foley, 1999) can have an important learning dimension:

> *Practically every community action initiative – from parents pressing for day-care facilities or a safe street crossing, to villagers attempting to build an irrigation system, to tenants' groups presenting schemes for rent reform, to demonstrations against local industry's intentions to build a car park on public play space, to campaigns for a nuclear freeze – exhibits a strong educative dimension in that the adults involved are engaged in a continuous process of developing skills, acquiring knowledge, and reflecting on their experiences, mostly in collaboration with other adults.* (Brookfield, 1986: 159)

Other studies have demonstrated that membership of voluntary groups and organisations can also generate a significant amount of valuable learning (Percy *et al*, 1988; Elsdon *et al* 1995). My own studies of the impact on parents and carers of active involvement in pre-school groups (McGivney 1998b and 1999b) revealed that it frequently leads to the development of new knowledge, understanding and skills although none of the people interviewed described this process as 'learning'. It was, nevertheless, learning of an extraordinarily rich, dynamic and transformative kind which, as well as enriching their family and social lives, had empowered many individuals and encouraged them to enter formal education, employment and engage in a range of other local voluntary activities.

This kind of learning, much of which may be an incidental by product of another activity, is often labelled 'informal learning'. It is not usually defined or recognised as learning partly because people tend to have a narrow conception of learning as something formal, structured and assessed. In an account of a pilot project mapping community opportunities for older learners in Leicester, Jones and Swanton (2000: 21) comment:

Of the many {learning} opportunities unearthed, mainstream providers deliver relatively few of them. (...) Participants' perceptions of the activities they undertake rarely include mention of 'learning' as a component.

However, this does not diminish its value or importance:

Learning is an activity that most people don't understand. It's often embedded in another activity of which learning is just one component: fishing, for example. There is a lot of very interesting adult learning that is not provided by local learning organisations, for example in housing associations and health action zone. Real learning is using learning to improve the way you do something, for example, regenerating a neighbourhood. This kind of learning – informal and reflexive learning – is often learning to support another activity. (Interviewee)

Adult learning patterns also reflect wider social and cultural changes. As argued convincingly by Field (2000), collective non-formal learning has diminished in importance over the last 20 years. This is associated with the decline in membership of voluntary organisations and the reduced influence of trades unions and left-wing political parties which had fostered learning for self-improvement and enlightenment based on 'collective identities and pursuing agendas of social change'. According to Field 'structured' adult learning has become more individualised, with much of it focused on leisure activity and individual self-improvement (sports, fitness, alternative therapies, self-help, ICT) – none of which may be identified as 'real' learning by the people concerned.

Thus, the actual amount of adult learning that is conducted may be considerably under-reported in surveys, as a result of which a large proportion of respondents may be negatively and inaccurately described as 'non-learners' or 'at risk' groups although they may be leading a life that is actually learning-rich. Moreover, adults tend to move in and out of learning in an apparently haphazard way, rather than participating in the neat, consecutive and linear manner that is expected – and desired – in policy. A significant proportion – nearly 30 per cent – of those classified as non-learners in NALS reported learning in the follow-up study *Pathways in Adult Learning* (Lavalle and Finch, 1999).

Nevertheless, the available data suggest that there are still many adults who are unconvinced of the value of organised learning, especially those who have had few positive experiences of it in the past. In all the NIACE surveys, the vast majority of respondents who claimed to have done no learning since full-time education said they were unlikely to engage in learning in the future. In the NALS survey, half of those who said they had not engaged in learning in the previous ten years indicated that nothing would induce them to do so. Thus some feel we have made very little progress in the last decade:

If you look at adult participation, we've been climbing a mountain and not making particular progress. I don't think we've made any real inroads into participation and non-participation. We haven't moved forward in ways we though we would in the early 90s. (Interviewee)

What can explain the apparent resistance by large sections of the British public to participating in *organised* learning activities?

What has fixed the pattern?

Chapter 3

Policy factors

It is generally accepted that a range of factors – practical, psychological, cultural and structural – interact to inhibit participation in organised learning. However, the implication in many policy papers and reports is that non-participation is often the result of personal inadequacies, lack of motivation or misconceptions about the potential benefits. The stress on individual learner psychologies downplays the powerful roles economic, social and political factors – all of which are largely out of individuals' control – have played in shaping adult learning provision and participation patterns over the past decades. Ascribing non-participation in formal learning to individual inertia or lack of motivation:

> *frees the formal system from blame for any part in low participation rates(…) glosses over the limited access that many workers (…) have to formal training at work and (…) transfers the problem onto those least fitted to respond* (Coffield, 2001)

There is an assumption in policy that if only people would act in a certain ways – i.e. adopt the behaviour and participation patterns of middle-class groups – problems of poverty and exclusion will be eradicated:

> *The inclusion/exclusion debate defines the problem of poverty and lack of access to social and economic resources as being about the dysfunction of particular groups in those communities. The solution offered in this model is for these people to adjust to a taken-for-granted middle class norm of behaviour, such as re-training, to enable integration.* (Stuart, 2000: 27)

> *Are we saying, as long as you are like the rest, you're ok?* (Interviewee)

This view opens the door to strategies to coerce people to participate in learning, something which, as documented by Field (2000), is already beginning to happen as can be seen in current pilot projects in which unemployed people judged to have literacy needs are obliged to engage in basic education programmes or lose their benefits. Preece (2000), however, sees the root of non-participation residing not in individuals but in the infrastructures, power relations and dominant values of society which conspire to exclude and give outsider status to people who do not conform to middle-class behavioural norms.

Patterns of participation are influenced not just by personal dispositions and preferences, but by prevailing economic and labour market conditions which create income disparities and differential access to resources, and by policy measures which shape the nature and supply of opportunities available and the conditions for gaining access to them:

> *The structures which are currently in place impact profoundly on lifelong learning in practice, since they enshrine in legislation and through funding mechanisms what may or may not be learned, by whom and under what circumstances.* (Sand 1998: 27)

Looking back over the last decade it can be seen that the drive towards lifelong learning has to some extent been neutralised by the exclusionary effects of policy.

The impact of policy on participation patterns

The number and rapidity of the changes introduced by successive governments to post-compulsory learning structures and funding systems have had a significant impact on the progress – or lack of progress – made towards achieving wider participation, although this is rarely if ever acknowledged by those actually involved in making policy:

> *Non-participants are often blamed for their situation, and threatened with exclusion, since the alternative of admitting the existence of socio-economic determinants for non-participation might require a totally different, and rather more expensive, government programme.* (Gorard, 2000b: 190)

During the 1980s, concerns about skill shortages and Britain's poor qualification levels led to an increasing policy emphasis on training and skills development. As Hillage *et al* (2000) relate, there was a pronounced shift towards vocationalism, accreditation and accountability. Local authority funding was reduced and the public funding of adult learning opportunities became increasing biased towards those with explicit instrumental objectives. At the end of that decade there were 'already (...) signs that the curriculum in some areas [was] shrinking towards more instrumental, vocational and Euro-centred programming'. (McGivney, 1990: 182)

Many of the policy measures and developments introduced between the mid-1980s and mid-1990s continued and reinforced this trend, notably the establishment of the National Council for Vocational Qualifications (NCVQ) and development of national vocational qualifications (NVQs); the establishment of the Training and Enterprise Councils (TECs) and their equivalent in Scotland, and the launch of the Investors in People programme (IiP). While these measures were partly informed by a concern to engage more people in training in order to increase their skills, a principal aim was to make employers and individuals shoulder more of the costs of provision, as was expressed explicitly in the Department of Employment paper *Strategy for Skills and Enterprise* (ED, 1993) and in the consultation paper and subsequent policy document on Lifetime Learning (DfEE 1995 and 1996):

> *The thrust of the Conservative government's lifetime learning project was to try to persuade employers to take on more of the responsibility for, and costs of, training at all levels, perpetuating what was, even by the government's own measures, a failing voluntarist approach. At the same time, individuals were exhorted for the sake of the nation's economic competitiveness to improve their 'individual commitment' to learning, but with no additional public investment and no real understanding of what might genuinely motivate learners or create learner demand. Learning is constructed as purely instrumental. Couched in the language of business and the market place, the {Lifetime Learning} report is addressed almost exclusively to employers and individuals to deliver the lifetime learning project. Publicly-funded providers of further and higher education are almost entirely ignored, since the need to constrain public expenditure was a higher policy priority than investment in education and training.* (Sand, 1998: 20)

An early and major casualty of these tendencies was the Inner London Authority (ILEA) which had made huge strides in making adult education accessible at very low cost (£1 a course) to groups disadvantaged by class, income, race, gender or age. The abolition of ILEA in 1990 was a severe setback to the cause of widening participation:

> *When ILEA went, the professional momentum that had built up went with it. A tremendous body of expertise was lost both on the basic skills and AE side. In ILEA there was a big cadre of staff who were experts. So many good things were lost. ILEA had great after-school centres. These were largely cut, then along came TECs and produced about three pathetic schemes for after-school provision, and we had government ministers coming along to open them as though these were some great new thing! Meanwhile, not far away, I was having to close down schemes because all the public funding was going into schools.* (Interviewee)

During the 1990s, the prioritisation of accredited and vocational learning continued. This trend was reflected in two significant and symbolic developments: the decision in 1994 to mainstream non-vocational continuing education courses provided by higher education institutions, with funding allocated to those leading to or carrying credits towards a recognised award; and the merging, in 1995, of the

Departments of Education and Employment (a short-lived marriage that recently ended in separation after the General Election of 2001).

The emphasis then was still strongly on skills (later in the decade this changed to 'employability' but has since reverted to skills). In 1994, the Economic and Social Research Council (ESRC) launched a new programme, *The Learning Society: Knowledge and skills for employment*, the aim of which was to examine the nature of a learning society and to explore the ways in which it could contribute to the development of knowledge and skills for employment and 'other areas' of adult life.

Some consider that the attempts in the early 1990s to raise skill levels, to link education and employment, to expand higher and further education and create new qualification routes, had the generally positive impact of 'gingering up' the system:

> *Ironically there was a huge growth during the Tory period. It was quite a creative period for both positive and negative reasons. There were great leaps forward – growth in HE (though bought at a terrible price); national targets; attempts to raise vocational education; NVQs; understanding of the relationship between children's aspirations and the world of work (TVEI); the need to seriously engage with the world of business; and the TECs – they didn't succeed but at least they raised issues.* (Interviewee)

However, while the emphasis on skills training and vocational education resulted in the creation of some new adult learning opportunities, the overall effect was a narrowing of the scope of adult provision, with government priorities firmly focused on work-related education and the younger adult cohorts. As Hillage *et al* (2000) remind us, the White Paper *Education and Training for the 21st Century* (DES/ED, 1991) proposed the withdrawal of public funding for all but 'useful' learning, an approach that caused considerable debate and controversy at the time and which, though subsequently watered down, influenced some of the measures contained in the 1992 Further and Higher Education (FHE) Act.

The Act ushered in major structural and funding changes, notably, incorporation of colleges, the establishment of the Further Education and Higher Education Funding Councils, the ending of the binary divide in higher education, with the former polytechnics becoming 'new' or 'post-92' universities, and the division of the adult curriculum into Schedule 2 and non-Schedule 2 provision.

These changes had a powerful impact on post-16 opportunities as well as on adult participation patterns. One result was a significant increase in recruitment of people aged over 19 into formal learning institutions – a trend that has continued:

> *Recruitment of adults became even more attractive to colleges in the deregulated competitive environment that followed removal from local authority control in 1992, not least because the new funding regime meant that resources followed student numbers (provided that they were enrolled on prescribed types of programme). By the late 1990s,*

adults were a clear majority of the FE college population, at least in England where some 80 per cent of students on publicly-funded courses were aged 19 and over. (Field, 2000: 41)

From the point of view of *wider* participation, however, the impact of the Act was mixed.

In some ways the Act specifically set out to widen participation. The newly established Further Education Funding Council, for example, was expected both to promote access to further education 'for people who do not participate in education and training but who could benefit from it' and 'to have regard for the needs of students with learning difficulties and/or disabilities.' To achieve these aims, two committees were set up: one, chaired by Professor Tomlinson, to review further education opportunities for students with learning difficulties and/or disabilities; the other, chaired by Helena Kennedy QC, to encourage more people to participate and succeed in further education. The reports produced by these committees *Inclusive Learning* (FEFC, 1996) and *Learning Works* (Kennedy, 1997) have both made a considerable contribution towards changing attitudes and practice in the further education sector.

The Tomlinson report proposed the influential notion of 'Inclusive Learning' – a process whereby institutional procedures and practices are fitted to learners rather than learners being expected to adapt to institutions.

Central to all our thinking and recommendations is the approach towards learning, which we term 'inclusive learning', and which we want to see adopted everywhere. We argue for it because it will improve the education of those with learning difficulties, but believe it is also true that such an approach would benefit all (…)

Put simply, we want to avoid a viewpoint which locates the difficulty or deficit with the student and focus instead on the capacity of the educational institution to understand and respond to the individual learner's requirement. This means we must move away from labelling the student and towards creating an appropriate educational environment; concentrate on understanding better how people learn so that they can better be helped to learn; and see people with disabilities and/or learning difficulties first and foremost as learners. (FEFC, 1996: 3)

Since the Tomlinson report was published, colleges have been able to claim additional FEFC funding support for students with learning difficulties and/or disabilities (SLDDs) as well as for a staff development programme to help them implement the proposals, and the general view is that considerable progress has been made in this area.

FEFC has done sterling work around widening participation with students with learning difficulties and/or disabilities. The advances of the last 10 years have been phenomenal. The way in which colleges deal with SLDD issues is now on the agenda of governing body meetings in ways they never were before. (Interviewee)

The Kennedy report *Learning Works* (1997) has also had a strong impact on policy and practice. The report recommended that learners should have an entitlement to learning on their own terms: 'unless participants get what they want, where they want it at the right cost, we will not get the widening of participation to the degree needed' (p9). It also called for increased funding for the further education sector and for a new system of funding that would allow for the additional costs involved in catering for learners from under-represented groups.

A number of the recommendations made in the report – with the notable exceptions of the introduction of an adult learning entitlement and 'learning pathways' – were acted upon. Overall funding for the sector was increased and a widening participation factor was introduced into the funding methodology to compensate for the higher costs involved in recruiting and retaining students from postcode areas identified as having high levels of socio-economic deprivation. Other direct consequences of the report were the setting of new learning and participation targets; the dedication of some lottery funding to learning; the expansion of childcare in further education; increased use of new technology for learning; and the establishment of 54 FEFC-funded strategic partnerships set up to identify learning needs among excluded groups, promote learning and stimulate creative responses. The latter, according to an interviewee, helped to prepare the ground for subsequent forms of local collaboration and:

turned happily and easily into lifelong learning partnerships. People by then had accepted that data-sharing was a good idea and that it was sensible and practical to work together on widening participation issues. For us it was also a critical underpinning of the UfI hub because we had all the necessary data. The data sharing was new and very important because without it we had no benchmark information on neglected areas. Policy sharing came out of that.

For me there's been a direct flow-on from Kennedy – a stress on widening participation, understanding of what's going on locally and this has fed through into local partnerships. That has been very powerful.

Many feel, therefore, that the Kennedy report has made a strong contribution to the cause of widening participation in learning:

Kennedy made widening participation respectable. (Interviewee)

The positive thing post-Kennedy, is that the locus for widening participation has moved from LEAs and Adult education centres to colleges. (Interviewee)

What a difference the Kennedy recommendations have made! (FE informant)

Many if not most FE colleges are more aware of their communities than back then {in the 1980s}. Adult education has moved centre stage for them, and many college practices have changed, usually for the better. (Taubman, 2000: vi)

Other consequences of the 1992 Act, however, were less benign.

The new funding mechanism

The national funding methodology introduced by the 1992 Act can be seen to have had both good and bad effects on adult participation. On the positive side, it encouraged colleges to offer provision for groups they might not otherwise have catered for. The mechanism also provided funding units to compensate for the costs of childcare and the additional support needed by some learners:

It contributed significantly to widening participation because it was a national funding regime. The ways in which colleges managed to manipulate and use funding schemes was a very welcome development. Those parts of the country which hadn't focused on this {widening participation} were given an opportunity to do so, particularly for people with learning difficulties and/or disabilities. (Interviewee)

Other aspects of the funding methodology, however, worked against widening participation.

Colleges were encouraged by the system to secure as many funding units as they could through recruiting full-time students on longer courses. This led to some discrimination against part-time learners studying for less than a certain number of hours per week, and against those likely to take a longer time to achieve specified learning targets.

It is often in an institution's interest to offer courses which require attendance just above the 15 hour mark when attendance below this level is precisely that which is often required by adult students because of their social, family and economic circumstances and the lack of financial support. (Uden, 1996: 46)

Outcome-related funding – a feature of FEFC (and TEC) funding methodologies – put an emphasis on 'progression' and qualifications, creating a situation in which education and training providers were tempted to give priority to the candidates most likely to achieve:

One of the negative things has been the straitjacket of FEFC, project or TEC funding having to lead to specific outcomes. TEC funding and measurement of outputs has resulted in skewing student intake. Value for money criteria doesn't always work. Some avoid FEFC funding because you can't have a time-scale on these people. (Interviewee)

In some respects the FEFC funding system militated against recruitment of new student groups. As only the gaining of qualifications or progression to other education or training counted as 'achievement', institutions lost funding units if students left programmes without completing courses, even when they had gained employment. The loss of units for non-completion inevitably acted as a disincentive to enrol students with social disadvantages or learning handicaps:

For many of the students who need to be attracted if participation is to be widened, 'drop out' is not always a function of factors over which the institution has any control (social and economic pressures, problems of unemployment, the lack of discretionary awards). The institution which has taken the 'risk' of widening participation to students who are disadvantaged by these factors is therefore penalised. (Uden, 1996: 47)

The new funding system also encouraged competition for students between institutions and this meant that catering for groups unlikely to attract the highest funding units shifted down colleges' priorities:

The greatest impact {on adult participation} over a decade has been incorporation across the board with funding and inspection systems that supported it. It led to a massive introduction of market forces – a crude market forces system – driving down the unit of resource more and more, and an inspection system which was superficial and looked at outcomes in very crude terms. Within this you obviously looked for students who get the best results. (Interviewee)

Several community workers reporting to my project on informal learning (McGivney, 1999a) also pointed out that the funding regime had resulted in a reluctance on the part of providers to refer people to more appropriate provision in other centres or institutions. As one put it, *'It can be a financial disadvantage if individuals move on and they want to hang on to their numbers to get funding'*.

In some ways, therefore, the new regime required FE institutions to act like businesses but at the same time they were expected to provide a public service responding to the needs of a range of different learners (Kennedy, 1997). These roles were mutually incompatible and it is not surprising that some of the institutions that ran into severe financial difficulties in the 1990s were those which were most active in working with local communities and targeting the more educationally disadvantaged groups:

The task of seeking to widen participation {is} left to those who because of commitment, lack of success in the prestige stakes, or geographical location, do not devote all their energies to expanding their market share of 'safe' students. Unfortunately, these institutions under the current arrangements are likely to be operating from an increasingly weak base and could be the first to suffer during increasing financial stringency. (Uden, 1996: 49)

Inevitably the most vulnerable groups were those most affected by the changes. One of the findings of a NIACE project on the impact of the FHE Act on adults with learning difficulties (Joseph Rowntree Foundation, 1996) was that, as institutions became competitive businesses, there was a reduction in collaboration with a subsequent loss of overall planning and coherence in catering for this client group.

The Schedule 2 divide

From the point of view of widening participation, one of the most detrimental effects of the 1992 Act was the separation it created between 'Schedule 2' courses designated as eligible for funding from the further education funding councils (mainly courses leading to qualifications or offering progression in education or employment, described at the time as 'national priorities') – and non-Schedule 2 'leisure' courses which remained the responsibility of Local Education Authorities (LEAs). This distinction:

> *established an artificial set of boundaries (…) between 'vocational' provision leading to qualifications (or preparation for qualifications) (…) and 'non-vocational' provision, not leading to qualifications, While this distinction (…) might conceivably make sense for 16-19-year-olds for whom post-16 credentials increasingly form the basis for selection and progression, it made no sense at all for adult learners either in mid-career or re-entering the system, requiring the kinds of responsive and flexible learning opportunities described by Kennedy. (…) Market demand from adults for qualifications designed for 16-19-year-olds is not high.* (Sand 1998: 28)

It was not just a question of demand, however; it was also one of supply. Local authorities were required to ensure 'adequate' provision of non-Schedule 2 provision, but as the notion of adequacy was never defined, and their priority was to cover the costs of supporting local schools, this (deliberate) vagueness predictably had a detrimental effect on LEAs' ability to continue offering varied and affordable local adult education provision:

> *For more than a decade central Government has encouraged Local Education Authorities to reduce discretionary areas of expenditure to reallocate money to schools. It is unsurprising that many authorities, as a result, cut back on investment in community based adult learning – the 'non-Schedule 2' curriculum. The result has been that for many pensioners, and others whose learning aspirations relate to personal development*

and cultural enrichment, there has be a marked diminution in curriculum offer, as funding priorities have led providers to skew the balance of offer in many localities. (NIACE, 1999: 1-2)

Although the new system had some positive effects – notably the securing of some forms of provision for adults – it simultaneously put back the cause of widening participation by leading to an overall reduction in provision of low cost, non-accredited learning opportunities for adults – a loss that particularly impacted on older learners, as well as to a reduction of initiatives designed to identify and respond to the learning needs of groups under-represented in organised learning activities. Not surprisingly, many providers were tempted to convert existing programmes designed to attract such groups into more formal accredited ones that would attract FEFC funding. Funding needs became more important than learner needs and this had an inevitable knock-on effect on wider participation:

It was no surprise when, through the 1990s, tutors helped the government by turning poorly funded uncertificated work into accredited, and therefore better financed 'Schedule 2' provision. That migration was bought at a high price. Between 1991 and 1994 NIACE mapped a forty per cent fall in older learners' participation. Few learners in their eighties are attracted by the romance of an NVQ3.

The Act was perhaps the high water mark of the drive towards utilitarianism in education policy – certainly as far as it impacted on adult learners. (Tuckett, 2001a)

Schedule 2, according to an interviewee, 'crystallised accreditation as an issue'. The emphasis on courses leading to accreditation and progression inevitably discriminated against those sections of the population such as older adults and adults with learning differences for whom accreditation is not always appropriate, as NIACE work in this area has consistently found:

As one person said forcibly: 'it's accreditate, not educate!'. The demands of accreditation sometimes skewed the learning process towards paper work and inflexible pre-set goals. (Joseph Rowntree Foundation, 1998)

The prioritising of instrumental and accredited learning inevitably led to a diminution of development work in local communities as well as to a decline in innovative approaches, for example in adult literacy work. (Eldred, 2000). Many of those working with under-represented groups found FEFC funding too inflexible. Those who had adapted their work to obtain funding felt they had lost some of the flexibility and student-centred ethos of their original programmes because of requirements to do with student numbers and predetermined outcomes, both of which can be difficult to achieve with some groups of adult learners (McGivney, 2000a).

Curiously, at the same time as the emphasis on learning for instrumental purposes was restricting and impoverishing the range of publicly-funded opportunities, opportunities based on a more generous notion of learning were opening up in the private sector, in workplaces with radical employee development schemes:

There was a blue-collar liberalisation {of AE} happening in the private sector at the same time as the opposite was happening in the public sector. Interesting how in a company like Ford where people clocked on and clocked off, you get learning redefining the relationship between the company and the workers. This was an interesting 1990s form of what was happening in Castleford[1] in the 1980s. Ford EDAP {Employee Development and Assistance Programme} was showing the value of learning for its own sake just as public bodies were becoming convinced that education for pleasure had little right to public subsidy. (Interviewee)

The loss of 'first-rung' non-accredited provision that resulted from the FHE Act is now recognised to have been one of the biggest impediments to widening participation during the last decade:

Public policy has concentrated strongly in recent years on providing education and training which leads to qualifications. This has led to a significant mismatch between the provision that is available and what is actually needed (Policy Action Team on Skills, DfEE, 1999b: 11)

A related effect was the loss of expertise in widening participation. Many experienced, community-based practitioners left the adult education field and this is considered by some to be one of the most negative results of the Act. After 1992, it became a major hurdle to justify public expenditure on time- and labour-intensive, community-based approaches which could not guarantee rapid and easily measurable outcomes. Providers wishing to attract and work with under-represented groups generally only had access to finite, year-on-year or short project funding requiring repeated and time-consuming bidding processes: 'From the 1980s onwards you were filling out forms for applications. Pump-priming money was available but nothing for the core.' (Interviewee).

The 1992 Act is therefore seen to have weakened adult and community provision and, consequently, affected participation – in a number of ways:

Firstly, it divided adult education provision into Schedule 2 and non-Schedule 2 with an indication that the first was essential (...) and the second was not. Secondly, it reduced the amount of adult education which was overseen by a democratically elected LEA rather than by a quango – the Further Education Funding Council – and thus its

---

1 Women's education centre started by miners' wives after the miners' strike.

community responsiveness. Finally, the Act failed to provide a definition of the word 'adequate' in relation to non-Schedule 2 provision and thus left it open to individual LEAs to decide on how much or how little adult provision they would provide in their area. This has resulted in extremely variable patterns of non-Schedule 2 adult education provision across the country and thus inequity in terms of access for adults to part- time study. (Hodgson and Spours 1999:11)

In terms of widening participation the Act combined a number of contradictory and somewhat self-defeating thrusts – a move to increase and improve learning opportunities that was severely handicapped by the artificial boundary imposed between different kinds of learning; an emphasis on specific learning outcomes that succeeded in intensifying the exclusion of already excluded groups, and a move to encourage collaborative provision at the same time that the establishment of separate funding councils and quality arrangements were 'creating new boundaries between the sectors' (Parry, 1997). Moreover, measures to promote educational progression, albeit well-intentioned, managed to confuse two very separate arguments, the second of which managed to gain the upper hand:

The first was that it wasn't right to leave students in ghettos and that you needed to offer pathways; the second was that education is only justifiable if you progress. But this is a separate argument. (Interviewee)

Post-1992 developments in HE

Despite the expansion brought about by the Conservative Government, higher education had remained a largely elite sector:

In the past wider participation simply wasn't an issue or on the agenda. It was in fact a non-decision, a consequence of structures. If you have so many people applying for places then you go for the most able and promising ie. the middle class. (Interviewee)

The end of the binary divide in Higher education following the FHE Act may, paradoxically, have brought about an even greater binary divide in so far as it has led to a tendency for the older universities to preserve their elite status by continuing to select students with traditional A-levels rather those entering by different routes:

{It} prompted a wholesale rush by all universities to re-position themselves in the HE marketplace with 'old' universities seeking to do so through research excellence. Alongside such a mission goes a strong identification with and investment in traditional academic standards and an elitist culture of 'selecting out' students in contrast to a widened provision concentration on 'selecting in'. (Johnston and Croft, 1998: 14)

This situation has led one analyst to enquire: 'what then should we do? Bus the 'disadvantaged' out of our area to the nearest university of inclusion?' (Whaley, 2000: 137).

As outlined in Chapter 1, although Access courses, franchising and more flexible entry procedures, together with the government-led expansion of the sector, stimulated an increase in the numbers of mature students, women, people with disabilities and students from ethnic communities, the highest proportion of these so-called 'non-traditional' students are to be found in the 'new' universities – a situation found also in Scotland (Bamber *et al*, 2000). Research indicates that working-class people are fully aware of the hierarchical divide but feel that their choices are limited to post-1992 institutions. 'They recognised that the "best" were dominated by white middle-class cultures and therefore "not for us."' (Archer and Ross, 2001)

Another factor that impacted on participation was the fact that the rapid expansion of the sector that was encouraged by the Conservative government took place with minimal extra resources. This meant that many of the core facilities and services needed to support new learners such as personal tutor schemes and counselling services, were reduced, which is likely to have had an impact on retention rates. The ending of the mature student allowance also had a negative impact on the recruitment of low-income mature students (see McGivney, 1996).

As in further education, however, some measures were introduced which had the aim of promoting wider participation. In 1995, funding for non-award-bearing programmes was made available to higher education institutions on a competitive bidding basis by the Higher Education Funding Council. Subsequently, following the publication of the Dearing Report (NCIHE, 1997), the issue of widening participation became a priority, with funding made available by the Higher Education Funding Council to support moves to encourage applications from a wider mix of people. The irony, highlighted by Ward and Steele (1999), was that this coincided with the ending of the former Continuing Education grant (which had funded in-house Access and other non-accredited courses), the phasing-out of maintenance grants and the introduction of student loans: 'Mature students from lower-class backgrounds were on the one hand invited to 'participate' but simultaneously deprived of the wherewithal to help them do it.' (p194)

Some of the changes imposed on further and higher education during the 1990s were characterised by haste and confusion. The expansion of the sectors was, in both cases, somewhat abruptly curtailed. A three-year period of 'consolidation' in relation to full-time enrolments was imposed on higher education in 1994, and the further education sector which, from 1993, had been urged to recruit more learners, franchise courses and provide more off-site provision, was also instructed to halt expansion in 1997 because the Treasury could no longer afford the demand-led (funding) element (DLE). This left a number of colleges in a difficult financial position, as had the policy of 'convergence' funding – a move designed to reduce disparities in the funding of individual colleges. Some feel that the latter measure was pursued without appreciation of the historical reasons for differential funding levels, some of which were to do with having more expensive (in terms of support) student clienteles. These developments caused some colleges to withdraw from the work they were doing with non-participant groups in the community (Uden, 1996).

Taken as a whole, therefore, despite various initiatives intended to broaden the composition of learners, many of the policy measures implemented during the 1990s resulted in perpetuating the conventional adult learner profile and, together with developments such as the removal of the statutory obligation on ITV to provide educational programmes, put back rather than furthered the goal of wider participation. Indeed, the consequences of some aspects of policy can be described as disastrous for those sections of the population already poorly served by existing adult learning opportunities. The kind of low-cost, informal local provision most likely to attract new groups into learning became an endangered species and, since the early 1990s, there have been great pressures on those wishing to recruit and work with groups under-represented in the mainstream. They have been forced to comply with certain criteria relating to enrolment, retention and outcomes and have encountered problems with 'number crunching' and producing proof of 'progression' interpreted mainly as enrolling in mainstream and acquiring qualifications:

> *There's been a bureaucratic frenzy with justifying what we do. Wherever you go there is this element of statistical measuring. But how do you evaluate the non-definable outcomes such as attitudes, spin-offs to communities and families?* (Informant)

The irony is that pressure on achieving numbers seems to have been stronger in development work and outreach programmes than in mainstream, despite the well-established finding that work with new learner groups can rarely produce outcomes such as high enrolment numbers, qualifications and educational progression within the short time-scales in which it is invariably conducted.

The drive to accredit, measure and standardise has also led to the over-formalisation of some adult programmes such as Access courses, which, as Sargant and Tuckett (1997) have commented, can create another barrier to participation. Moreover, the instrumental focus of policy in the 1990s may have had a subliminal impact of public perceptions of educational programmes. Ronayne (quoted in Owens, 2000) suggests that making employment initiatives more attractive than educational ones may implicitly convey a message that other learning opportunities are of lesser status and value. This may explain why people do not always report less formal courses in research studies and adult learning surveys.

Throughout the 1990s as a whole, there was little official recognition and support for informal non-accredited learning. It was, as Tuckett (2001b) describes, 'a bleak decade for community-based adult learning [when] budgets for uncertificated adult education were remorselessly squeezed'.

Reduction in workplace learning opportunities

One of the paradoxes of the last decades has been that increased public investment in the expansion of learning opportunities has been accompanied by a decrease in the supply of workplace learning opportunities as large manufacturing sectors have declined and there has been a shift from larger companies to smaller ones (Gorard, 2000b). Many people get their major adult learning experiences in the workplace. Data from the International Literacy Survey (OECD, 1997) suggested that employer-supported learning is a critically important source of post-compulsory learning in the UK, more so than in any other participating country except the USA (Rubenson, 1996). Inequalities in employer support for learning may therefore have much to do with the under-participation of certain groups:

The analyses show that the likelihood of an employee receiving some support for education and training from the employer is related to the size of the company that one happens to be working in, occupational status and the engagement in literacy activities at work. In general it is a handicap to work in a small to medium-sized company (...) Persons outside the labour market or in undemanding jobs are clearly up against a barrier with regard to both learning itself and their readiness for it. (Rubenson, 1996: 261-262)

Although there has been repeated evidence that certain groups of employees – those in smaller firms, part-time workers, those in manual occupations and older workers – receive little employer-supported learning by comparison with other groups (McGivney, 1994 and 1997), a major flaw in the widening participation agenda of the 1990s was the failure to introduce measures to persuade employers to provide more opportunities for the most excluded workers.

Disparities in student funding support

Another reason for the continuing imbalances in the learner profile has been the unevenness and inconsistency of financial support for students. There has been little financial support available for part-time learners and arrangements for student support and institutional finance in both further and higher education have been based on the assumption that typical learners study full-time. This has discriminated against adult learners, the majority of whom learn on a part-time basis. The continuing bias in favour of full-time students has also helped to maintain the social class profile of the student body and reinforced the tendency for those with most existing educational capital to take advantage of existing opportunities.

There have also been disparities in the support available to those studying in different sectors. In their study of financial support for students in further education, Herbert and Callender (1997) found that the latter were the 'poor relations' of higher education students both in terms of access to funding and in terms of the type and level of financial support available, despite the fact that their financial need was likely to be greater. The investigation revealed that funds were not distributed according to notions of equity or need and their receipt was often discretionary, dictated by the decisions and policies of a range of gatekeepers. Moreover, learners facing hardship were treated very differently according to their age, their place of residence and the courses followed.

Herbert and Callender itemised the weaknesses of the various sources of financial support available to learners in further education. Discretionary awards from LEAs had become a lottery and their availability depended on where students lived or what they studied; Access funds were highly discretionary and offered low levels of support; fee exemption and remission did not cover indirect costs and student maintenance; employer support was very unevenly distributed, and the Job Seekers' Allowance was an insecure form of support because of the 16-hour study time rule and the requirement that unemployed claimants remain 'available for' and 'actively seeking' full-time work. In addition, European funding was not always sought or secured by colleges, and Career Development Loans and tax relief for vocational training did not succeed in attracting the most financially disadvantaged.

The authors concluded that the system of financial support in further education was unfair, confusing and full of anomalies, and therefore likely to perpetuate the social class and age profile of the student body:

> *The system favours young, full-time, academic learners while penalising adults, part-time and vocationally-oriented learners (...) The funding system in Britain for further education students is totally inadequate and unfair. In its present form, it is likely to have only a minimal impact on widening participation.* (pp xiii and xv)

A subsequent report on student support arrangements in further education (DfEE, 1998a) voiced similar concerns, namely that:

- the availability of financial support varied in different parts of the country: students in the same circumstances and with the same needs were not entitled to receive the same support.
- expenditure on discretionary awards for further education had been reducing dramatically since 1992 and was still falling.
- there was virtually no financial support available to students after age 18. Adults

could study part-time while in receipt of the Job Seekers' Allowance but many had to leave their course to take a job when one was offered.
- There was a lack of clarity and consistency about people's entitlement to state benefits when they were in education.

The Benefits System

Most reports on barriers to learning produced in the 1990s comment on the fact that the Benefits System was deterring unemployed people from engaging in structured learning.

A study of the effects of the 16-hour study rule (Donnelly, 1997) typically found that unemployed people who wished to study were frequently prevented from doing so. This was partly attributed to the complexity of Benefit rules and regulations and the wide variations in the ways these have been interpreted and applied. The study revealed inconsistent operation of the rules by different benefit offices and staff members; different definitions of full-time and part-time courses; and disruption of learning programmes because of compulsory interviews and government programmes.

* * *

What is clear from this brief overview is that policy directions in the 1990s had a push and pull effect on widening participation. As noted in *Education's for Other People*, this phenomenon was already apparent at the end of the 1980s:

> *Some developments in the further and higher education sectors appear to run counter to the general momentum towards increasing access for non-traditional students. The steady cuts in universities' finance and staffing over the last decade, together with proposed cuts in the numbers of lecturers in further education and public sector higher education, suggest a service that is shrinking at the same time that it is being required to expand.* (McGivney, 1990: 181)

Judgments on the last decade have been mixed. According to one interviewee, the overall direction has been a positive one, especially towards the end of the decade:

> *I feel fairly positive about the 90s because widening participation became respectable; because there was progressive attrition of some of the most instrumental and economistic arguments about education. At the beginning of the decade every policy paper re-ran the debate about economic benefits, then personal and social benefits – that irritating division – then from that low point, it 'softened' and there was a greater balance that culminated in that magnificent rise in Blunkett's preface.*

Other analysts, however, take a more pessimistic view. Some feel that the thrust of policy during the 1980s and most of the 1990s had a generally detrimental effect on adult learning:

> *Far from facilitating lifelong learning, the 1992 Further and Higher Education Act, the establishment of separate funding councils for further and higher education, the setting up of the Qualifications and Curriculum Authority (QCA) and the 'reform' of the 16-19 qualifications system subsequent to Dearing's recommendations, constitute between them a profound and fundamental impediment to the implementation of any real agenda for lifelong learning and the participation of adults in the learning process, particularly those who are currently under-represented.* (Sand, 1998: 28)

> *A succession of governments focused on the needs of the labour market for a supply of flexible, skilled labour, and too often ignored any passion for learning or mild curiosity that resisted codification, accreditation, or other measures that provided external benchmarks. The complexity of funding mechanisms, at least in further education, took away many of the best minds from teaching and learning and engaged them in harvesting funding units. A parallel process in higher education saw extra-mural programmes dragooned by funding streams into a concentration on credit bearing courses. Clearly there have been winners in this exercise, as can be seen from the decline in the number and proportion of people in the workforce who possess no qualifications and from the steady rise in participation of those who enjoyed an extended initial education. But there have been losers, too. The overall participation pattern showed that it did not pay to be old or poor, if you wanted to learn for its own sake, and this despite targeted fee waivers, and a growing recognition that something needed to be done about what the CBI called 'the long tail of under-achievement.'* (Tuckett, 2001a).

Policy, then, has played a large part in maintaining the traditional patterns of adult participation in post-16 education and training over the last decade. But what about the post-16 system itself? What are those who do not engage in organised learning expected to participate in?

Chapter 4

Supply and institutional factors

Complexity

The diversity of post-16 education and training can cause confusion for potential learners, and the succession of reforms of the last decade, albeit often instigated with the aim of simplification, may have intensified rather than reduced the complexity.

There is no doubt that post-16 education and training is a seriously messy affair, characterised by a huge variety of programmes, qualifications, organisational contexts, delivery arrangements and funding schemes. Many people consequently have difficulty finding their way around the range of provision, qualifications and fee levels:

> *Rather than being given access to a clearly defined and easily understood 'seamless robe' of provision or ladder of progressive learning opportunities, the potential life-long learner is confronted by a range of competing autonomous institutions, often offering similar types of courses, but with a bewildering range of qualifications outcomes which do not automatically ensure access to a higher level of study (...). There is often no-one to help the learner to find her/his way through the maze of programmes and qualifications on offer.* (Hodgson and Spours, 1999: 4)

In this respect little has changed over the last decade:

> *Post-compulsory education is complex, fragmented and diverse. Professionals working in one part of the system often have little knowledge or understanding of the others. It is unrealistic to expect the public to understand the system if educationists themselves have little sense of the whole.* (McGivney, 1990: 175)

The language and presentation of prospectuses and course directories can compound the problem even for those ready and able to enter a programme of study. In research with adult learners in Worcestershire, members of focus groups commented on the confusing language, especially the use of jargon (Dinsdale, 2001).

The qualification system is often singled out as particularly confusing for would-be adult learners and the establishment of new frameworks and awards may well have accentuated the problem for those entering further or higher education:

The Qualification Framework consists of eight so-called levels (in effect confused with years of study (…). If we look at the two systems together, then from the point of view of lifelong learners, attempting to access learning opportunities in response to their identified learning needs across a range of levels, for a variety of different purposes, what is being proposed is extraordinarily confusing, guaranteed to deter the most motivated of learners. What a learner is presented with appears to be a complicated, twelve level qualifications framework within which the important interface between further and higher education levels is unclear, where different types of qualification appear to have a different status, where comparability of level is difficult to ascertain, and where different elements of the system are funded differentially on the basis of quite different methods and principles. From the learner's point of view, both curriculum and funding distinctions are not only irrelevant but constitute a major barrier to participation(…)The two frameworks seem to have been designed quite independently of each other (…) Neither of them has been designed to take account of, or in any way to seriously engage with, the lifelong learning agenda or adult learners. (Sand 1998: 32)

Uneven distribution of learning opportunities

Some communities may not have participated in organised learning simply because there have been no or few opportunities locally available. For a long time (and it is not yet clear whether the Local Learning and Skills Councils will remedy this) there have been wide disparities in the geographical spread of education and training provision as well as in the amounts spent on widening participation work by different providers. These variations have been under-explored,

Farr (2001) argues that research into widening participation often also ignores the geographical location of institutions. This could be an important consideration, over and above quality and subject choice, for an increasing number of students:

Almost all of the coverage which makes reference to postcodes talks about them in relation to their socio-economic make-up and the participation of that socio-economic 'type' within higher education. Very rarely is the distance from that postcode to the nearest university or college considered and, more importantly, the variety of universities or colleges available within a reasonable commuting distance of that postcode. (…) As the numbers of people applying increases it is likely that a greater and greater proportion will need to consider the trade-off between what is available at an institution and how far from home that institution is. (pp17-18)

Economic and social differences between regions mean that policy measures can have a significantly different impact on different localities. However, Rees *et al* (1997) point out that although national changes in the structure of learning opportunities have been experienced most acutely in local contexts, there have been few attempts to relate changes in patterns of educational participation to regionally- and locally-specific processes of social and economic development:

> *Not only have many policy changes been implemented primarily at the local level, but also the interaction of national policies with local conditions has produced highly variable local outcomes. For instance, the national policy of expanding learning opportunities for younger adults through Youth Training in reality had very different effects according to the local context; and this is reflected in wide differences in take-up, completion, and eventual outcomes for young people(...) There are complex interactions between people's locations within the social structure, their spatial locations and their access to learning opportunities.* (pp 491- 492)

Rees *et al* observe that provision of learning opportunities has been strongly affected by changes in the economy. Over the last decades there have been considerable changes in local and regional economic circumstances with growing disparities in the demand for skills. The changes to industrial structures and employment opportunities brought about by national and international economic developments have had a differential impact on local labour markets and this has influenced local provision of education and training, as illustrated in South Wales where colliery closures led simultaneously to loss of jobs and loss of training opportunities. The researchers suggest that the effect of local labour market developments on the participation patterns of different adult groups has also been insufficiently appreciated or researched.

The differences in local labour market conditions lead Gorard (2000a) to question the assumption implicit in lifelong learning policy documents that we are progressing from a situation in which there were few opportunities to learn, to one in which there will be more and better structured learning opportunities. He argues that the opposite is true in places like south Wales where industrial decline and local economic changes have led to an actual decline in learning opportunities.

Uneven distribution of workplace opportunities

There have also been wide disparities in the education and training provision offered or supported by employers, with those most disadvantaged in the labour market generally receiving least (Robertson, 1997a; Callender, 1999). Despite innovations such as Investors in People, surveys have consistently revealed that professional and managerial employees are significantly more likely to have received employer training than semi-skilled and unskilled occupational groups, while older workers and those in smaller firms are particularly poorly provided with workplace learning opportunities.

Surveys consistently indicate that training for the least qualified and skilled workers is very patchy with most provision biased toward the workers who are already skilled and in higher grade occupations. According to the Spring 1998 Labour Force Survey, only 13.5 per cent of plant and machine operatives received job related training compared to 46.4 per cent of professional workers.

> *Access to training is individually cumulative and socially divisive. The higher the level of qualification, the greater the likelihood that an individual will receive further training (…) For employees locked into the impoverished training environment of small firms, prospects for career development and enhanced qualifications are bleak in comparison.* (Robertson 1997a: 7)

Green (1999) points out that although the quantity of work-based learning increased during the 1990s, the length of training episodes actually dropped – a situation confirmed by analyses of Labour Force Survey data (Gorard, 2000a).

Employer failure to provide training has been identified as a strong contributory factor in our national failure to achieve wider participation and a culture of lifelong learning:

> *Employers appear unconvinced of the need to invest in the skills of their own employees. Whatever criticisms might be directed at individuals with little motivation to learn, or at successive administrations seemingly obsessed with spending money only on initial education, it is apparently British private and multi-national employers who are the weak partners in this lifelong learning venture at present.* (Gorard, 2000a: 6)

Uneven distribution of opportunities for the most under-represented groups

The uneven overall distribution of adult learning opportunities has been paralleled by an uncoordinated and patchy overall approach to provision targeted at the groups least represented in education and training. Despite national measures and incentives to encourage education providers to cater more for excluded groups and communities, there continue to be huge disparities between localities and institutions in the quantity and quality of the programmes developed for such groups. This was illustrated in a NIACE project to explore and describe examples of continuing education for groups with learning difficulties (Joseph Rowntree

Foundation, 1998). The study revealed an overall scarcity of provision nationally, and found that existing examples of provision were 'fragile' and vulnerable to cuts. Lack of staff awareness of learner needs posed a major barrier, as did the quality of student support. Other problems identified were lack of physical access for people with mobility difficulties, transport problems and inaccessible information. The study also found that some staff working with these groups faced opposition from managers and had to justify their work as important and necessary, meriting dedicated resources and staffing. Finding appropriate provision was particularly difficult for those with more than one 'label' to contend with (for example Asian women with learning difficulties).

Other groups have fared equally badly. During the last decade there has been a particular lack of attention to the learning interests and needs of older adults, despite their increasing numbers in the population: *'the participation of older adults is very patchy and it's the usual story: it is down to individuals rather than policy decisions and those individuals are not championed'* (Informant). A mapping exercise into fourth-age learning commissioned by the DfEE found some examples of good practice but an overall inconsistency: a few examples of good practice and strategic thinking *'contrasted sharply with an overall lack of any meaningful activity of reasonable quality'* (Soulsby, 2000: 23).

An audit of provision for other traditionally neglected groups would almost certainly reveal a similar patchy and uncoordinated picture, with initiatives often depending on the availability of special funding or the interests and commitment of specific members of staff.

In recent decades some of the most imaginative and effective widening participation initiatives have been initiated *outside* the education system – for example, Castleford Women's Centre in Leeds, started by miners' wives; the former Women's Education Project in Northern Ireland which was funded largely by charitable sources, and employee development schemes which started as partnerships between unions and employers:

> *So much doesn't start with the education system. Some of the most innovative and radical ventures were not originally supported by education.* (Interviewee)

Disparities in fee levels

In addition to the uneven spread of learning opportunities, there have been considerable differences between areas in the fee levels charged to adults by further education, local authority and community education providers, as well as in the availability of financial support for disadvantaged learners. Whereas people over 19 not on means-tested benefits have been charged about 25 per cent of the cost of vocational programmes, those enrolling in adult and community learning programmes have often had to pay most or all of the costs involved, depending on where they live. The main public support for adult learners has been through reduction or waivers of fees but again, this has varied between locations and providers. A survey of fee levels charged by colleges and local authorities in 1998-99 showed that, as in previous years:

> *Where people live continues to be a very significant factor affecting both the range of opportunities to engage in learning as an adult and the price of that learning. Arrangements for fee concessions continue to vary widely, and frequently, significantly affecting people's chances to learn particularly for those whose freedom to 'shop around' is affected by low income, age, disability or lack of transport.* (Aldridge, 2000)

It is to be hoped that the new post-16 structures will eliminate some of the disparities and inequalities that characterised fee levels during the last decade.

Institutional factors

It is widely accepted that the ethos, characteristics and practices of education institutions have played a large part in the non-participation of certain groups of the population over the last decades. The exclusionary effects often start with very basic things – confusing and untargeted promotional literature; intimidating buildings which lack a clear main entrance and enquiry point; brusque and unhelpful responses to enquiries, unanswered telephones or failure to reply to messages left on answering machines, complex and lengthy enrolment forms and entry procedures; lack of harmonisation between learning arrangements and people's other commitments.

Such factors which were noted in *Education's for Other People* have continued to deter people from approaching an institution or enrolling in a course of study (Queen Mary and Westfield College, 1999; Dinsdale, 2001). In my earlier study of informal education, a community education worker on a large estate reported that an unsatisfactory first contact with an educational institution deters not only individuals but also their network of family, friends and acquaintances: 'if it is not a good experience the word spreads immediately'.

For many people, however, the strongest barriers erected by institutions have been structural and embedded in culture and tradition. This applies particularly to higher education where:

> *The inequitable nature {of institutions} in terms of habit, culture, regulation and*

finance continues to constrain the participation of many segments of the population, particularly those in the inner-cities. We may have moved from an elite to a crowded, some would say 'mass' system in numerical terms, but we have not yet established the preconditions for a popular and democratic higher education for the next century. (Robertson, 1997b: 27).

Since the early 1990s, further education institutions have been obliged to adapt rapidly to changes in policy, funding and working conditions and, in terms of widening their intake, 'had to wake up pretty fast', according to one informant. Higher education institutions have been slower to react and change their practices.

Varying degrees of commitment to widening participation

At the end of the 1980s I found that the providers who were trying to create opportunities for a wider cross-section of the community were doing so for a variety of reasons – ethical, because it was a matter of social justice; practical, to fill empty places or increase the numbers of students; opportunistic, because special funding was available, and (frequently) a mixture of the three (McGivney, 1990). I concluded that equity was rarely a primary goal of the larger education institutions. An impressionistic view suggests that this situation is broadly the same today although the second and third reasons for widening participation cited above are perhaps more prominent because of government targets and the new funding streams now available for the purpose of recruiting a wider constituency of learners. One therefore has to question the genuineness of some providers' commitment to the cause of widening participation as opposed to gaining additional funding.

Even now in a political climate that actively promotes wider participation, the need to change the profile of adult learners is not totally accepted. In their report on widening participation in colleges, FEFC (2000) noted that about 10 per cent of colleges and other providers of further education indicated no commitment to widening participation in their mission statements.

The commitment to wider access in some higher education institutions is also in doubt, especially in those universities and subject departments where there are no problems with recruitment·

Widening participation here is considered 'a good thing' but some departments would rather it happened somewhere else! (Informant)

The first 'league tables' indicating universities' relative success in recruiting students from disadvantaged background showed that in Autumn 2000, 10 – nine of which were Russell institutions – had very low benchmarks and nine failed even to meet these.

A report on widening participation by the Higher Education Funding Council (HEFCE, 1996) suggested that remedying social imbalances in participation was outside the sector's power as it is something that should be dealt with earlier in the educational process. Robertson counters this complacency by pointing to the exclusionary impact of higher education policies and practices for which institutions themselves are responsible.

According to some reports many of the pre-1992 universities are reluctant to change their entry criteria based on 3 good A-levels to accommodate people with different qualifications. Bamber and Tett (2001: 8), for example, cite research findings showing that the 'more elite' universities feared that the inclusion of a broader, less qualified, 'high risk' cohort of students would threaten academic standards, and require more resources than were readily available. However, Robertson (1997b) claims that the dominant elite in higher education could be manipulating the standards agenda to preserve their position:

> *the creation of 'degrees of difference' – reputational gradients between institutions and credentials – is one way by which élites preserve their privilege.* (pp17-18)

Robertson suggests that this reflects a wider societal ambivalence about wider participation which sometimes leads to subtle and not-so-subtle hurdles being put in the way of achieving it:

> *As fast as the Access movement has opened up opportunities for personal progression and success, elite groups have found new ways of protecting their offspring from the effects of the erosion of the 'credential gap' on labour market prospects. The sterile pursuit of 'standards', and the suborning of credit frameworks for this purpose, are just the latest tactics in this longstanding war of attrition between the 'restorationists' and the 'modernisers' in post-secondary education, reflecting battles in society more widely.*

> *Access to higher education (. . .) challenges the prevailing balance of forces in society more widely since it de-monopolises access to the most prestigious forms of educational capital – higher credentials. Those social groups whose advantage has hitherto been closely connected to their access to these credentials are bound to resist their wider availability and will seek to enlist a favourably-disposed government in their efforts.* (ibid)

Some institutions therefore make no effort to construct access pathways or support structures for learners who do not conform to their conventional student profile:

> *It is difficult to attract new students when the University, despite much prompting, has as yet no articulated policy of progression to degree level for {them} nor any systematic way of recognising the different needs and circumstances of adult or part-time students in the University as a whole.* (Johnson and Croft, 1998)

Lack of articulated progression routes has also been an obstacle to wider participation in further education. One study (FEDA, 1995) found that there were few structured progression routes from informal adult education into institution-based Schedule 2 provision.

It is not just formal institutions, however, that fail to encourage movement between different providers and sectors. It has been found that some informal, community-based providers develop a group ethos and sense of solidarity which leads to over-protectiveness and a reluctance to refer learners on to other learning providers:

> *In the past, their orientation has often been to sustaining participation within their systems rather than moving students onwards and upwards. Providers and participants alike may have suffered from a fear of letting go of the supportive situation which they were providing or participating in.* (Munn *et al*, 1993: 18)

> *The downside relating to people who are very good at {widening participation} is that they become over-protective of their patch.* (Interviewee)

Marginality of widening participation initiatives

The ambivalence of some institutions towards attracting new groups of learners is reflected in the status of the work targeted at them. The extent and nature of institutional involvement in community-based outreach has been extremely variable (McGivney, 2000) and the continuing imbalance in the social composition of learners in many institutions has often been 'structured in' by the marginal and under-resourced nature of the measures ostensibly initiated to rectify it.

The built-in marginality has often been (and is still) reflected in the physical location of the work. One informant concerned with widening access claimed that her work is 'always in the portakabin at the back', and it is also noticeable that widening participation centres or units in some large institutions tend to be on the edge or furthest reaches of campuses.

> *On the periphery – with low status teachers and learners. Many colleges will take you out to huts at the extreme ends of their campuses and that's where these people will be.* (FEFC inspector quoted in McGivney, 2000)

> *We need the best facilities for these groups but too often they get everybody's leftovers.* (Interviewee)

According to Bellis, Clarke and Ward (1999), the greatest difficulties in widening participation work arise when projects are both physically isolated and do not have the visible support of senior management. The marginality of such work is, however, often pre-determined by central funding which labels it as an 'initiative' and often focuses on activities outside rather than inside institutions. Hoy *et al* (2000), for example, point out that the widening participation invitation-to-bid documents from the Higher Education Funding Council in England listed 12 areas of activity likely to receive funding, the majority of which were:

> *likely to be located peripherally to the higher education sector such as improving networks, credit frameworks, advice and guidance and outreach activities. There is little advice as to the sort of projects (apart from staff development) which might influence strategies for transforming the mainstream and enhancing students' learning experiences.* (p154),

As this suggests, there are limited understandings of what is meant by widening participation. According to FEFC (2000a), colleges often understand it as relating only to remedial programmes. Many also see it as an access issue rather than a process involving satisfactory participation and achievement. Although there is increasing awareness that widening participation should involve successful learning, the FEFC survey found that most colleges fail to set targets and develop strategies to improve achievement rates among under-represented groups.

The lack of priority attached to widening participation in some institutions – which often stems from the way in which it is funded – has been reflected in the status of the workers most involved in trying to achieve it, many of whom have been appointed to low status and often short-term positions. The contradiction at the heart of so many widening participation initiatives has been that those who are most effective at doing it have invariably been the least secure and lowest paid workers, often on temporary and fractional contracts. The work that probably requires the most highly developed and complex skills in all post-compulsory education – development work among diverse social and ethnic groups and disadvantaged communities – is often the least recognised and rewarded. My study of outreach (McGivney, 2000) found that a high proportion of the people engaged to do development work designed to widen opportunities for different community groups were appointed on a part-time and short-term basis, on a year-on-year budget basis or for the duration of funding for a project or initiative. Consequently, much of the widening participation work conducted by adult, further and higher education providers has been a separate, isolated and marginal process.

Lack of integration with mainstream

The widespread failure, noted in *Education's for Other People*, to integrate widening participation initiatives with mainstream work continued throughout the 1990s.

Although a number of influential reports and policy documents stressed the desirability of widening participation, few also stressed the need to adjust the mainstream practices and procedures of education institutions in a way likely to achieve that goal. According to Sand (1998), for example, while the Dearing report called for a different constituency of learners to have access to higher education, it did not recommend any corresponding changes in traditional structures and procedures, therefore implicitly assuming *'the perpetuation of a selective and stratified system'* (p24). In many institutions, therefore, activities targeted at under-represented groups have been restricted to fragmented, short-term special measures that have usually been outside of and unconnected with the mainstream. As a result, there has been little long-term impact either on the overall student profile or on institutional practice.

> *A great weakness (…) has been the relative marginalisation in the past of these special attempts to widen the scope of participation while mainstream institutions have continued, even when they have been expanding i.e. increasing participation, to provide in their traditional ways for those who wished to participate. Specially funded, time-limited projects were often allowed to demonstrate success and then expire.* (Hillage *et al*, 2000)

Unsupported transitions

Some further and higher institutions have also perpetuated exclusion by maintaining traditional selection procedures, structures and funding mechanisms established for a traditional, younger, full-time student body despite the transformation of the student age profile:

> *The weakening of the age-based entry criteria has transformed the student population in some central traditionally youth-oriented institutions. However, it has yet to transform large areas of institutional practice. Many FE colleges in England, and some universities, are now effectively adult education and training institutions. But far from reinventing themselves to meet the needs of their new constituencies, universities and colleges have made relatively minor incremental adjustments.* (Field, 2000: 42-43)

As a result, the participation of individuals who manage to overcome multiple barriers in order to access those institutions can be far from easy. For middle-class people already habituated to formal education, the process can be relatively straightforward. For working-class people, however, it can be a difficult and alienating experience (Bamber and Tett, 2001). As Jennings (1995: 17-18) suggests, the experience of entering formal education is far more difficult for new groups than for adults who have moved in and out of formal learning contexts throughout their lives, 'who experience little discontinuity in the assumptions and expectations about learning'. For, as observed by Ball *et al* (2000),

> {*...in entering HE} the risks and reflexivity of the middle-classes are about staying as they are and who they are. Those of the working-classes are about being different people in different places, about who they might be and what they must give up.* (p23)

The difficulties can also be acute for people who make the transition from informal community-based learning to a formal learning environment. Research in Coventry (McGivney and Thomson, 1995) indicated that the culture gap and the differences between the levels and demands of courses provided in community organisations and education institutions are sometimes great. The flexibility and student-centred style of courses as well as the support provided in community-based provision – help with finance, childcare and bilingual support – are not always matched in formal education institutions, many of which have resisted incorporating the features of effective outreach work into their mainstream practices because of conservatism or 'unsupported fears' that community education initiatives are a threat to quality (Whaley, 2000).

The way an institution responds to different groups of learners has a strong impact on their retention and achievement levels as suggested by a study by the Learning and Skills Development Agency (Davies and Rudden, 2000). This found that some further education colleges with high numbers of students from lower socio-economic groups had a high proportion of students gaining qualifications whereas others with similar student profiles had poor achievement levels. After comparing student groups in the colleges with the highest and lowest achievement rates, the researchers concluded that less than half the differences in achievement could be attributed to the student profile therefore the different performance levels must reflect differences in institutional ethos, systems, procedures and practices as well as demographic and other factors outside the direct influence of the colleges concerned.

Although some progress has been made since 1990 and Tomlinson's concept of inclusiveness has made a difference, people from non-participant groups entering formal education are still expected to adapt to the institution rather than institutions adapting to suit them. As Chisholm (1998) has memorably observed, 'Innovation is demanded of individuals, whereas institutions are simply left to continue to behave as they always have'.

Many have remarked on this dichotomy:

> *The focus is on the learner's ability to fit into the system rather than the capacity of the education offered by the institution to be inclusive. The outsider status of these learners is attributed to factors such as a lack of motivation to participate on their part, little*

encouragement from peer group and family, financial constraints, and fear of failure.

An exclusive focus on supporting the individual student to overcome these constraints and to cope with the demands of the institution implies benign neutrality on the part of the wider educational system in creating this situation and a benevolence on the part of the tertiary institutions that are willing to accommodate these learners as exceptional cases. (Ryan, 2000: 46-47)

Although there has been growing recognition of the support needs of new learner groups in terms of guidance, finance, childcare, study skills, and so on, these have rarely been sufficient to meet actual needs and part-time learners in particular have often been poorly provided with support. The FEFC (2000a) report on widening participation and raising standards in further education found that part-time learners and those in community-based provision were least likely to receive tutorial support.

Reinforcement of 'difference'

Another way in which institutions have hindered wider participation is by perpetuating and reinforcing the 'outsider status' of new student groups through the language they use (Ryan, 2000; Hoy *et al*, 2000). For example, negative labels such as 'non-traditional' and 'non-standard' are often applied to groups of learners who enter mainstream education by learning routes other than A Levels. Woodrow (2001: 8) refers to a 'mixed bag' approach to new learner groups in HE which brings together a wide range of people – young people from low income backgrounds, minority ethnic groups, refugees, single parents, unemployed people and women returners 'into a single category under the collective label of "non traditional" – all measured against the standard norm of the white, middle class students with good A levels.'

As Ecclestone (2000) argues, the stereotyping of under-represented groups is undermining efforts to widen participation:

In place of uplifting images of learners are negative images of those who do not want to participate. A seminar on 'non traditional students' in HE presented a long litany of characteristics that 'these people' are likely to have: broken homes, parents without qualifications or jobs, lack of self-esteem, lack of a "learning culture' at home.

In a conference about widening participation in FE 'the disaffected' were portrayed as likely to be illiterate, single parents, living in isolation, unable to help their children with homework, having poor self-esteem, prone to poor health and depression, poorly motivated for learning and lacking social skills. (...)The danger is that labels turn complexities into platitude. Increasingly it seems that anyone who doesn't participate in learning must be "dejected" and "disaffected".

The categorisation of new participants according to various labels of disadvantage reinforces differences between them and the traditional middle-class learner body.

The sense of difference or marginality felt by new learner groups is accentuated if there are few staff from a similar culture or background to their own. There is evidence that the ethnic and gender profile of staff and students in a centre or institution can have a strong impact on enrolment patterns (McGivney, 1998a). The absence of senior staff from some ethnic minority communities has long been a cause of concern. A recent staffing audit conducted by an independent commission for black staff in FE revealed that black people compose three per cent of lecturers and five per cent of support staff. There were only two black principals and very few black managers (Tysome, 2000b).

It is also worth mentioning the current dearth of staff with the appropriate experience and skills in working with different and disadvantaged groups of learners. Implicit in discourses about widening participation is an assumption that education and training providers have the capacity and expertise to conduct the kind of work that will engage new groups in learning. However, the policies of the early 1990s – cuts in local authority spending and the changes brought about by the 1992 Further and Higher Education Act – led to the loss not only of a substantial amount of community-based work but also of many of the practitioners skilled in doing it:

One thing was neglected during the 90s: we didn't appreciate the human resource issue in relation to teaching staff. We thought there were enough skills around but now we're facing a person crisis: people aren't trained in the important widening participation skills. In policy terms we didn't realise that we needed to address this. (Interviewee)

Many providers now have little concept of what is involved in community-based learning. There has also been a dearth of training in widening participation approaches not only for development workers but also for tutors who are not used to working with new groups of students or working in non-institutional settings. Some of the further education managers interviewed for my outreach study (McGivney, 2000) had found that teaching staff were struggling with these new responsibilities:

A problem is expecting our staff to go and teach on a range of locations. They aren't confident enough to do that, Delivering at a local level is very valuable and they benefit from it but it's hard to do if they haven't done it before.

It's a false expectation to expect FE lecturers at the front line to be able to deal with new groups. How can you expect our staff to deal with users who have never walked through the door? You'll never achieve inclusion just from the bottom up. There has to be top-

down bottom-up synergy. Unfortunately those at the top don't realise they have to change. I think all staff should have skills training on dealing with the disaffected, The sector needs tools for doing the job. Are we really taking on their needs?

There are, of course, wide variations in practice and some institutions have started to review their teaching and staff development practices in order to meet the challenge presented by a wider diversity of learners (FEFC, 2000a).

Curriculum

Another way in which exclusion is perpetuated is through the curriculum. Drawing on the work of Bourdieu (1993) and his notion of 'habitus', Bamber and Tett (2001) discuss the role that education institutions such as schools play in reproducing social and cultural inequalities form one generation to the next. Their research:

supports a view of schools as trading posts to which students bring different sorts of 'cultural capital'. Only some kinds of knowledge, dispositions, linguistic codes, problem-solving skills, attitudes, and tastes, get rewarded or valued by schools so those with the 'right' (i.e. legitimated) cultural capital fare the best. (p10)

This situation continues in post-16 education where what counts as relevant and valuable knowledge in education institutions tends to be that contained in subject disciplines rather than the lived experience of people who are expected to leave their identity and interests at the door: According to Whaley (2000: 132), 'experience is not the recognised currency of academia and there is rarely an equitable exchange rate'. A number of other higher education analysts have noted that although piecemeal changes have been made in higher education to accommodate a wider mix of learners, there has been little challenge to the knowledge base:

What our students knew in abundance (...) often did not count as knowledge. Universities, as bastions of power, decided what 'real' knowledge was and admitted to it only those who met their criteria.

In the universities (...) knowledge was the focus, and students were admitted to partake of it, strictly on the institution's terms and only when they had overcome the many obstacles which defended the university from the outside world. (Malcolm, 2000: 15, 16)

Within the higher education sector to date, there is evidence of a marked preference for maintaining the existing educational delivery system and little evidence of a willingness to critique the knowledge base that informs this system. Participation in the system is conditional on conformity to predetermined truths, and dissension is suppressed. Under these circumstances engaging with learners who have experienced peripherality is tantamount to intellectual colonisation.

The opportunities and constraints that impact on the establishment of relationships between peripheral communities and formal educational systems have much to do with the fundamental differences in philosophical positionings of both and in the 'kinds of knowledge' valued by both parties. (Ryan, 2000: 51)

Mayo and Collymore (2000) wonder whether the purpose of widening participation in higher education is to transmit and reinforce existing norms and values or to promote critical reflection leading to social change. Their series of pointed questions challenges policy-makers and providers to reconsider the whole issue of curriculum in relation to wider participation:

Is the prime objective the attainment of 'useful knowledge' – instrumental skills and training – or 'really useful knowledge' which enables people to make sense of the hardships and oppression they experience in their daily lives and to develop strategies for greater equality and social justice. (...) Is the focus primarily economic or wide enough to include social, cultural and political aims and objectives? Is there the space for education for active citizenship, and is there room for the learning needs of those who may not be actively seeking paid employment (...) people with major caring responsibilities, or people recovering from mental illness (...)? And is the emphasis upon individual advancement alone or is there also room for group support and collective benefits for the local community? (p142)

This issue has been repeatedly ducked in the promotion of wider participation. In their observations on the report by the UK Select Committee on Education and Employment on access to higher education (2001), Thomas and Quinn (2000) comment that it is 'quite remarkable' in a document on education that:

at no point is there any reference to curriculum, to the knowledge which higher education is purported to develop and disseminate. Widening participation implies a trans-formation of what can and should be learned in HE, with a dynamic relationship between student and knowledge production. One of the most interesting and challenging aspects of access is the presence of new perspectives and standpoints brought by different groups of students. At no point in the report is this intellectual dimension addressed. The emphasis appears to be on facilitating entry into an unreconstructed system where values and academic standards are fixed and immutable. Thus a valuable opportunity to really explore the role and meaning of higher education in the 21st century is lost. (p5)

In other education sectors the instrumental and economistic emphasis of government support for learning over the last decade has also resulted in a situation in which certain kinds of learning are valued above others, with public funding largely restricted to the types of course perceived most likely to lead to outcomes such as qualifications and greater employability. This has effectively narrowed the curriculum for all except those with the funds to select programmes more attuned to their interests:

> *In so far as there is a problem about participation in adult learning, it is located in the apparent limited ability of formal providers of adult education and training to engage with the interests and enthusiasms of the adult population across a range of 'difference'.* (Forrester and Payne, 2000: 101)

There can, however, be a significant gap between the knowledge and skills valued by policy-makers and education providers and those valued and sought by excluded communities. This leads to perceptions of exclusion and a view of the formal education curriculum as irrelevant:

> *Lack of recognition of alternative knowledge or perspectives creates a sense of exclusion for minority or under-represented groups.*

> *Dominant values marginalise the values and experiences of different social groups. This marginalisation is reflected in the way education is offered through, for example, its curriculum and teaching styles.* (Preece, 2000: 7, 12)

The mismatch between community learning needs and what providers are willing or able to deliver has been a strong factor in perpetuating the middle-class adult learner profile.

Accreditation

During the 1990s, the question of what is an appropriate curriculum for excluded groups got lost in the preoccupation with accreditation – a situation that still largely obtains today. As one interviewee suggested: 'We've lost the notion of curriculum, accreditation is the issue, We have a fail or pass culture'. Although many people want and value it, accreditation is not appropriate for all groups of learners and its imposition can intimidate and deter those who wish to learn for other purposes (Merton, 1998; WEA, 1998). Thirty-seven per cent of respondents to a Campaign for Learning survey claimed that the stress on qualifications had put them off learning (Campaign for Learning/MORI, 1998). Some tutors have found that if accreditation is mentioned or introduced too soon it can give rise to anxieties about failure and constitute another 'hoop' for people to jump through.

As discussed earlier, however, the emphasis in national educational policy has long been on a vertical model of academic progression. The following were typical comments from some of the outreach and guidance workers consulted during the course of my study of informal learning (McGivney, 1999):

There's been a rush to accredit whether it's appropriate or not.

There's a problem of 'shoehorning' programmes to make them accreditable.

There's a question about fitting everything into a credit framework. It's not always appropriate and can create barriers. Not all learners are ready for or interested in accreditation.

Some of the community-based providers contacted during my project on informal learning (McGivney, 1999a) felt there were pressures on them to use qualifications they considered were inappropriate for the groups they were working with.

There is little doubt that accreditation, when optional and introduced with sensitivity, has given many new learners a great sense of achievement. When an obligatory element of programmes, however, it can prove a formidable barrier to participation for the groups most resistant to formal education:

The way to get people in is to show them that they can learn. You don't start by putting them through qualifications, etc. More informal leisure courses are important. You need to create spaces where they can take control and realise their potential in learning. If all you're interested in is qualifications, you'll cut them off. There is a danger that this might happen again with the LSC. (Interviewee)

*   *   *

To cite these issues is not to ignore or dismiss the huge strides made by providers in all sectors to recruit and offer appropriate opportunities to the most educationally excluded and disadvantaged groups. Many institutions have become far more flexible and inclusive in recent years and have succeeded in attracting people from many of the groups previously under-represented – although there has been 'a less rigorous approach to identifying those more likely to leave courses before completion or to fail to achieve their learning goals' (FEFC, 2000a: 9).

Some of the lessons from that good practice exemplify what can be done to change the pattern of adult participation.

Chapter 5

Personal and cultural factors

To stress the contribution of structural and institutional factors to non-participation is not to downplay the role of personal, social and cultural factors in decisions to engage, or not, in organised learning. However, the range of personal barriers people face to participation – those related to social class, economic status, age, gender, ethnicity, disability, and geographical location – have been frequently explored (see for example, Maguire *et al*, 1993; Maxted, 1999) and there is no need to rehearse them in too much detail again. The question here is whether there has been any significant change in the last 10 years in the nature and extent of personal barriers to participation that people experience.

There is little evidence to suggest that the personal and cultural factors that have deterred people from engaging in learning during the last decade are substantially different than they were during the 1980s. The reasons most frequently given for not engaging in organised forms of learning are still invariably the practical ones to do with immediate circumstances – level of income, time constraints related to employment and family commitments, ill health or disability, place of residence, lack of transport. These affect people differentially although some are widely experienced. Bowman *et al* (2000), for example, found that family responsibilities – especially childcare – still constitute one of the greatest barriers for people who want to engage in education and training. This is despite a number of recent policy measures to increase facilities for pre-school children.

Financial worries are another very common stumbling block for potential learners especially those wishing to take a more advanced course of study. Changes in financial support for students in higher education have resulted in a reduction in the number of applications from people over 25 (Thomson and Tysome, 1998) and have also deterred potential applicants from a working-class background. Recent research into the perceptions of those in social classes C2, D and E showed that finance was a key barrier to entering higher education: 'Fear of debt, resistance to loan repayment, the need to earn money and other financial responsibilities were cited as reasons for not participating' (Archer and Ross, 2001).

Financial problems have also had a negative impact on mature students in further education (Callender, 1999). Callender's study, which examined the income and expenditure of FE students, found that under 25 per cent of learners received any financial help towards their studies. Over 50 per cent of students experienced financial hardship, two-thirds had no savings and over a quarter were in debt. Those who suffered the most financial hardship were adults: full-time students over the age of 19, students from lower social classes, lone parents and couples with children. Callender found that these students had little knowledge and awareness of potential sources of financial aid. Over half had received no information about the costs before starting their courses; two in five had perceived the costs incorrectly, and a third had underestimated them.

Cultural, social and psychological barriers

Most institutional strategies to widen participation have been designed to remove the practical obstacles. Other personal barriers, however, are less easy to deal with. As was found in *Education's for Other People,*

> *the major barriers to participation are attitudes, perceptions and expectations, although life situations and material circumstances also play a crucial part. Attitudes related to social class and gender roles are particularly resilient and difficult to change.* (McGivney 1990: 175)

Nothing has happened in the last decade to make me change this view which has been confirmed repeatedly by other researchers and analysts:

> *When educational disadvantage is compounded by other material differences – of gender, ethnicity, poverty, class, disability and sexuality – the effect is often a denial of imagined possibility. Too often education has already written these people off, and they internalise a belief that education is not for the likes of them.* (O'Rourke, 1995: 111)

> *While beliefs, attitudes and behaviour could well be shifting, some long-held perceptions about education in general and higher education in particular are rooted very deeply in cultural and in family and school experiences.* (Tonks, 1999)

Gorard (2000b: 189) has commented on the role of long-term socio-economic background characteristics, especially the influence of families; 'in creating a learner identity which does not view current opportunities as appropriate, interesting, or useful'. He notes that this is often accompanied by additional personal factors – poor prior educational experiences, low achievement; unemployment, limited aspirations, low self-esteem, lack of confidence and lack of trust in 'officialdom'. People with these characteristics have often deduced from their background and school experiences that 'education' is a formal and divisive process that suits middle- and upper-class people far more than those from poorer backgrounds. As many children – especially those from working-class backgrounds – leave school at the earliest opportunity convinced of the irrelevance of education and its lack of connection with their everyday lived experience, it is hardly surprising that the social divide perpetuates itself beyond compulsory education.

Educational self-concept

As has frequently been observed, one of the strongest inhibitors to engagement in organised learning is negative self-perceptions in relation to learning arising from earlier school experiences. In their report on community attitudes to education and training, Bowman *et al* (2000) use the term 'educational self-concept':

> *to describe the way that interviewees refer to themselves, often using terms like 'brainy' or 'thickie' in terms of their beliefs about themselves educationally. The sense of educational failure and struggle that many of the interviewees discussed suggests that their perceptions of themselves educationally do not encourage them to enter education and training courses that may only serve to reinforce their negative self-concepts.*

> *It was not only those who had only just left school who associated adult and further education with school experiences. There were many interviewees over 19 who also talked about having problems with work and education in terms of their educational self-concept and their education history. This was somewhat supported by the notions that those who were participating in education had, that others thought of them as in some way remedial.* (pp19-20)

This theme recurs several times during the report:

> *The issue of educational self-concept is extremely important for those who have had negative experiences at school. In particular it can inhibit educational participation, especially when people have problems with literacy.* (p23)

> *Throughout all the interviews negative images of school were common. These included the rejection of desk-bound passivity associated with being told what to do; regulated and pressurised learning and teaching associated with examinations and achievement levels.* (p27)

Such feelings help to explain the unease many people still feel about using the word 'learning' to describe the activities they engage in, even if they involve a structured programme or course. It also helps to explain the resistance to participation that is often encountered in national surveys such as those conducted by NIACE:

> *When asked why they did not take part, or plan to take part, in learning, nearly two-thirds of non-participating respondents reported no actual barrier to their participation, suggesting that their patterns of behaviour would remain* (Gorard, 2000b: 189).

This resistance is often linked to outdated perceptions of the formal education sector. Colleges are still widely seen as catering exclusively for younger learners and higher education institutions for a professional elite. A number of studies (McGivney, 1990, 1992a, 1999c) have also found that many people automatically assume that the programmes provided in further and higher education are beyond their financial and intellectual reach and that qualifications are always required as a condition for entry.

Risks in participation

Policy discourses on lifelong learning imply that participation in structured learning is a relatively easy process, but this ignores the range of risks such a step would involve for many people. For those without experience of post-compulsory learning, engaging in education or training may seem a frightening leap into the unknown. It may also mean getting into debt, a possibility that can deter people from working-class backgrounds and low income groups. Among some Muslim communities, interest-bearing loans are actually proscribed (Piatt, 2001). The implications of this do not appear to have been fully grasped. According to Callender, who has produced several reports on student finances, policy-makers view loans as income whereas students view them as debt (Thomson, 2001).

It has therefore been found that the educational routes to what policy-makers consider as 'success' are difficult for many people to take:

> *A wide range of factors may play a part in affecting the ability of people to deal with work, education and training in a fashion which is considered as 'normal', or, at least, in the case of policy, is considered as typical. The community that was the focus of our study confronts its members with a range of risks that may reduce their capacity successfully to negotiate or even perceive their paths to 'success' in the worlds of work, education and training. The extent of the risks they face is a feature of the social structure. (…) Exposure to these risks appears to be a crucial determinant of the ability that people have to find their way through the broader systems of work, education and training. (…) These risks are not evenly distributed throughout society.* (Bowman et al, 2000: 27).

The risks are not only economic but also social and psychological: fear of failure, of not being clever enough, of being too old to attend an education institution, or of losing face among ones peers. Some male groups, for example, feel that participation in formal education may reflect badly on them and result in loss of face and status (McGivney, 1998a). There are also anxieties about leaving familiar territory and 'comfort zones', linked with fears about possible alienation from family, social networks and colleagues in areas and organisations where there is no tradition of participation in organised education.

For many people another risk is the absence of a guaranteed 'pay-off' from learning. Higher level study in particular requires a substantial commitment of time and finance and may involve considerable personal upheaval and disruption, for very uncertain returns. Thus it may not be a feasible option for those who have little knowledge of or faith in its potential benefits. As Piatt (2001) argues, higher education is a much riskier options for disadvantaged groups than for those from a middle-class background:

> *The rates of return carry little weight in the absence of successful graduate role models. A degree may be a sound investment but it's an unknown quantity for many young people. Uncertainty about standards expected at college and a profound lack of self-confidence compound the risk factor. The social and financial capital of the middle-class provides a safety net and a second chance in case something goes wrong. For students from disadvantaged backgrounds, the stakes are much higher.*

Focus groups recently conducted by the University of North London showed that working-class communities did not lack information or aspiration but that:

> *the reasons for non participation were located within multiple structures of inequality, with HE largely viewed as a risky, unknown option offering uncertain returns. Most acknowledged the potential benefits of university if it led to success but these were juxtaposed with the high social, economic and personal costs of participation and uncertain outcomes. Previous educational experiences meant that 'failure' seemed a likely prospect, but respondents also worried that the vocational or access qualifications which would provide their routes into HE might be a source of disadvantage.* (Archer and Ross, 2001).

Scepticism about the value of education and training

Bitter experience has already taught some groups that participation in organised education or training programmes does not bring any tangible rewards. Ecclestone (2001) refers to a project in the North East which has found that increasing numbers of young adults who have taken part in successive schemes and courses are failing to gain lasting employment:

> *If their efforts don't pay off, no wonder antipathy takes root (...) Setting targets for more qualifications will not resolve these dilemmas and technical changes to motivate people will have a limited impact.*

Dinsdale (2001) has also found that unhelpful career advice and training that leads nowhere can instil scepticism about the value of any form of organised learning:

> *Some men said they found Job Centres very intimidating. One man had wanted to go into sports coaching but was told there was practically no work available in that field but 'that factory work would suit him'. Another man reported 'I've done 3 restart schemes now and I still don't have a job, they just send you on training for the sake of it'.* (p3).

In some respects, therefore, there does not seem to have been much change since the early 1990s when unemployed people found that they were being corralled into unproductive training schemes mainly in order to remove them from the unemployment register (McGivney, 1992b).

Conforming to social and cultural norms

As noted in Education's for Other People, cultural norms and peer group dynamics have a very powerful influence on whether or not people participate in education and training. That study found that peer and reference group influence is particularly strong within some of the groups most resistant to engaging in organised learning (for example, male manual workers). Individuals in such groups do not readily depart from accepted values and norms. My subsequent studies of unemployed people (McGivney 1992b), women (1993), part-time workers (McGivney, 1994) and men missing from education and training (McGivney, 1998a) all confirmed how difficult it can be for individuals in certain communities, occupational groups or social networks to depart from cultural behaviour patterns. Moreover, as Field (2000) comments, people with many of the characteristics associated with low participation such as few qualifications and limited job prospects often live in family environments and neighbourhoods which 'offer few resources to promote an active embracing of lifelong learning'. (p148)

Bowman *et al's* (2000) research found that individuals' families and immediate networks sometimes actively discourage them from participating in organised learning by requiring them to adhere to established behavioural norms. They found that women and young adults in particular were strongly influenced by their families, local communities and broader networks in the options they felt were open to them and in the decisions they made. Young adults were strongly constrained in their behaviour by local and peer group mores and, as found in earlier French research cited in McGivney (1990), some married or partnered women seemed to have little control over their lives and very limited spatial and financial autonomy. Some had been forbidden by their male partners to speak to callers or to leave the home during the day. In some cases it was the male partners' families who applied or reinforced these restrictions.

A number of other studies have found that women often experience opposition to their participation in education from their families, especially their male partners. Those who do engage in learning can experience painful conflicts between the student role and their partner and maternal roles (McGivney, 1993; Hayes, 1999).

*   *   *

The personal and cultural barriers faced by many of the people who do not engage in organised learning seem to have changed little over the last decade. There also seems to have been little change in attitudes to education and perceptions of its usefulness. Is there anything we can do about this and will current policy measures make a difference? What strategies have proved effective in changing attitudes and participation patterns?

How to change the pattern

Chapter 6

Lessons from practice

What have we learned about widening participation over the last decade? What policies and practices encourage and facilitate the engagement of those least represented in organised learning programmes?

Some of the answers have been obvious for some time from existing evidence of good practice. As Tony Uden (1996) argued several years ago, we already have the necessary knowledge and understanding to achieve a more socially balanced profile of adult learners:

> *We have been here before. Through countless neighbourhood and local projects and campaigns and in the kinds of large-scale initiatives described {earlier in this study} the tools have been assembled.* (p60)

The analysis and many of the measures advocated in the Kennedy report on widening participation in further education (1997) chime with the experience of many who have been working in the field for the last few decades: 'As I first read Kennedy I kept thinking, "we did most of this 20 years ago!"' (Taubman, 2000: VI).

Similarly, the aspects of good practice listed in the FEFC Guide (1997) and reports on widening participation and raising standards (FEFC, 2000a and b) – measures such as effective outreach activities, provision of information and guidance, learning and learner support, appropriate curricula, mechanisms for recording achievements – have all been identified many times before, not least in *Opening Colleges to Adult Learners* (McGivney, 1992a).

The current policy emphasis on the need to provide 'first-rung' community-based learning programmes to attract those least represented in formal education and training (DfEE, 1999b) also confirms what has long been known. My study of adult participation in learning the late 1980s (McGivney, 1990) showed, repeatedly, that an effective way of engaging the most excluded groups was to provide informal 'first-stage' learning activities in familiar community settings, based on thorough preparatory groundwork and personal contacts. This was something which, even then, had already been clear for several decades:

> *When the first Social Exclusion Unit report came out there was little recognition of the work which had gone on using learning for community regeneration. That's changed now. People are now talking about the things we did in the 70s. There's a real sense of wanting to tackle exclusion – bottom up and empowerment – things we would have said needed to happen in the 70s. Now we're having to reinvent things like outreach and community-based provision. There's been a restoration since 1997 of some of the concepts that were pioneered in the 1970s. They have become part of Government post-16 education strategy.* (Interviewee)

In other words, we seem to have come full circle and many of the policy and widening participation documents since 1997, albeit valuable aids to the field, contain little in terms of ideas for widening participation that has not been known and advocated since the 1960s and 1970s.

> *I think that over 20 years we've ended up where we started, It's been a long hard road to get back to where we started. When I read Kennedy, I thought: hang on! We've done all this. How appalling it is that all that history, all that experience and all that practice was increasingly lost during the '80s and mainly during the 90s. It's a tragedy. A body of experience is completely lost.* (Interviewee)

From the viewpoint of the 21st century, therefore, few of the measures recently promoted and introduced for engaging a greater cross-section of the population in organised learning seem particularly new or revolutionary (with the exception perhaps of ICT initiatives). Indeed, given the substantial literature on access and participation that has been produced during the last three or more decades, it seems surprising that so much has *needed* to be rediscovered. However, national (and some institutional) policy-makers have repeatedly ignored the existing evidence on how best to attract and work with the least represented groups and there appears to be an assumption in current policy that nothing significant about widening participation in learning was known before 1997. As Ward and Steele (1999) comment, although moves to widen access have continued for more than a century, each new policy round seem inclined to forget what went before: 'successful but inevitably under-funded activities are allowed to founder while the wheel is rhetorically re-invented' (p192).

The consequence is that measures to broaden the pool of adult learners have often failed to draw on the lessons of the past. To give one recent example: according to an evaluation of Non-Schedule 2 pilot programmes, both the FEFC and individual colleges 'seriously underestimated' the long lead-in time that is required in developing these kinds of learning programmes (Greenwood *et al*, 2000). Yet the need for this is something that has been stressed repeatedly over the years by practitioners and researchers. Other issues that emerged from the evaluation have also been well-documented: for example it was found that to expect learners to progress to higher level (Schedule 2) courses was unrealistic, given the short time-scale of the projects. (Past evidence has frequently shown that movement from Non-Schedule 2 to Schedule 2 provision can take several years.) It was also realised that the learners who did move on to mainstream provision would encounter exactly the same barriers that the pilots had needed to reduce in order to facilitate their access in the first place – another situation on which there is substantial existing evidence.

Baseline principles

What this perhaps reassuringly indicates, however, is that despite the bewildering plethora of changes that has been imposed on the structures and funding of post-16 education and training over the last few decades, there are some constants in encouraging and achieving wider participation, even if they do need to be continually rediscovered. Now that we have a new post-16 structure and new people in policy-making decisions, these do need to be restated.

With regard to publicly-funded provision, for example, there are certain baseline principles that should be applied across the piece. These, to borrow from a consultation paper on the telecommunications industry (OFTEL, 1996), are: *geographic accessibility* – access to similar services on the same terms throughout the UK; *affordability* – fee levels that people can reasonably afford; and *equal opportunities* – measures to ensure that groups with particular constraints and needs have access to services. As argued in Chapter 4, the continuing disparities in the quantity and costs of learning opportunities offered in different areas have militated against living up to these principles over the last decade.

Removal of practical barriers

The salience of certain factors in attracting new learners and facilitating their successful participation is continually reaffirmed. The ways in which education and training provision is presented, its perceived relevance, what it costs, and where, when and how it is delivered – continue to play a crucial part in influencing decisions to engage, or not to engage, in organised learning programmes. A common strategy for attracting less-represented groups into learning programmes has therefore been to provide learning activities in ways that minimise the practical obstacles that inhibit their participation.

A notable example of effective practice was the raft of measures taken by the Inner London Education Authority (ILEA), before its abolition, to engage the groups identified as most excluded from the learning opportunities offered in the Adult Institutes. These included: minimal fees, a broader curriculum negotiated with groups in the community, sensitivity to cultural and language factors and flexible childcare and transport arrangements. These measures resulted in a significant increase in enrolments by women with caring responsibilities and people who were unemployed, without formal qualifications, from a manual background and from black and other minority communities (Uden, 1996).

The low fee policy (£1 per course) was particularly effective in attracting new learners. This is a finding that recurs with monotous, though unsurprising, regularity in research: 'it is beyond question that financial aid can widen participation in education, especially among low-income groups' (Herbert and Callender, 1997: XIII). A recent study has shown that more 16-year-olds, especially boys and young people from low-income families, are staying on in education because of the educational maintenance allowance (EMA) that has been made available in some pilot areas (Piatt, 2001; *Working Brief*, 2001b).

Learner-centredness

Time and time again, as in the ILEA, adult education practice has shown that the key to widening participation is to focus on the interests and well-being of learners rather than those of providers, and that the kind of activities and programmes most likely to attract groups who traditionally have not participated in post-school education or training are:

- offered in informal and non-threatening community venues
- free of charge or offered at low cost
- negotiated with learners and tailored to group or individual interests
- sufficiently flexible in delivery and content to cater for emerging interests and changing circumstances of learners
- offered with a range of support services such as childcare. (McGivney, 1990)

None of these were original findings even in 1990 and it is not surprising that their importance continues to be identified in research.

In NIACE research into the outcomes of informal foundation training programmes for unemployed people in Coventry (McGivney and Thomson, 1995), the same features were singled out with remarkable regularity by diverse groups of participants as key factors in helping them to complete courses and move to other purposeful activities. The frequency with which trainees identified them as contributing to their learning success indicated that it was far more than the focus of provision that was important – it was the whole 'package'. The learning environment, the general ambience and the support structures available were considered to be as important as the content and quality of the provision in raising levels of confidence and self-esteem; in relieving depression and isolation, and in helping individuals to make positive changes in their lives.

In the evaluation of Non-Schedule 2 pilots (Greenwood *et al*, 2000), the characteristics of provision listed above were again cited as the ones most valued by learners, together with other features that have also frequently been identified as important – small-group learning, approachable and understanding tutors, a short initial commitment, and learning about things in which people had a real interest.

Practice also shows that the first engagement needs to be relatively short and located within people's 'comfort zones'. Studies often report that, in some deprived areas, many people prefer to stay in familiar territory and do not readily go more than a mile or two from their homes. Recent research into community attitudes to learning typically found that some groups inhabit very 'geographically-bounded' communities:

> *made up of people in a small number of streets in a relatively small area; they did not cross major roads or traverse areas of open space. Although people had moved around the estate they tended to move within these street by street boundaries or to move further afield but travel back (...) in the streets where their major networks were based.* (Bowman *et al*, 2000: 23)

As many studies have confirmed, only very local interventions are likely to attract such people. As one informant put it, 'If they aren't comfortable in a place they'll walk'.

Removing the cultural and psychological barriers

You can, however, remove all the well-established practical impediments and still not succeed in attracting some groups. What then?

There are cultural, social and psychological factors which deter people from even considering engaging in learning, and there are practical and structural factors which inhibit their ability to participate when they are prepared to do so. Logically, the first set of factors comes before the second. People have to be ready or motivated to participate in a learning programme before they even consider the costs, whether they have the time or how to get there. However, the barriers to participation that are invariably mentioned first, and are usually addressed first, are the practical and external ones. You can remove these by making provision free, running it at flexible times and in local venues, providing childcare and using IT for those who cannot access conventional programmes. You can do all of these things, but you may still only construct half a bridge across the 'learning divide'. This is because the secondary barriers are being tackled instead of the primary ones which are much greater. These are people's expectations, perceptions and self perceptions:

> *The measures needed to motivate someone to be interested in learning, to encourage them to see the value in learning and to have the confidence to take part, may be quite different from measures designed to overcome a particular hurdle, e.g. cost, caring or transport.*
> (Hillage and Aston, 2001:11)

It is understandable that there is greater focus on the practical barriers. It is far easier to cite these as reasons for not participating than to admit to feelings of apprehension about education or lack of confidence in ones ability to learn. It is also easier for providers to provide solutions to practical problems than to psychological or cultural ones. But these are the obstacles that have to be addressed if we want to widen participation among those least likely to take advantage of the learning opportunities available.

So how do you change people's expectations and perceptions when these have been so strongly instilled by cultural conditioning and personal experience?

Pre-entry activities

My work on adult education issues over the years has repeatedly confirmed the necessity of investing in the pre-entry stage and conducting a painstaking process of familiarisation and trust-building with the groups who would not consider approaching an education or training provider. In the case of the most excluded groups, one of the best ways of changing attitudes and perceptions has always been to engage in a genuine dialogue with them and to respond to whatever interests and needs are identified. This involves, first, identifying and making contact with the communities that are poorly represented in existing provision. Many providers now do this as a matter of course although this sometimes does not extend much beyond leafleting and other marketing approaches. Local research may be necessary, although it is not always useful. Sometimes it just reproduces information that is already common knowledge. One interviewee referred to:

> *endless local research and no action. I don't think we need to know any more. A local college here spent a quarter of a million on widening participation and all they came up with was the scale of the problem. Why didn't they just get on and do it? Money could have been spent on provision. Researching 'need' is a total waste of money.*

However, some forms of local research can help to frame solutions. In Leeds, according to another interviewee, research in some local areas conducted by the City

Council Training Department revealed unexpectedly low levels of school attainment, court orders and offending behaviour and this led to the design of special pre-employment programmes for the groups concerned.

Group targeting

Targeting *individuals* in attempts to engage the most excluded groups is unlikely to be effective. It is often assumed that people make decisions about entering education and training as autonomous agents. However, research consistently indicates that this is not the case: family, social and occupational relationships play an extremely important part in people's lifestyle choices and directions:

> *{the stress on} individual motivation does not take seriously the fact that people do not calculate their own futures on their own and without reference to others. Indeed, the idea that people are free agents who can make their own decisions on these kinds of issues is misleading. In our study, family relationships and the restricted networks of 16-19-year-olds in particular, play a major role in influencing how and why people decide to participate in education, training and work...*
>
> *In our study social networks can be seen as the source of people's perceptions and decisions both to participate and not to participate in education and training provision.*
> (Bowman *et al*, 2000: 39)

As discussed in Chapter 5, people are very influenced in their behaviour by their peers and networks. From the point of view of engaging in learning, this can be a positive or negative influence depending on group norms and values. It need hardly be restated that members of family and social networks within which engaging in organised learning is a normal and customary activity are far more likely to participate than members of families and networks in which it is not a customary activity. Some groups of men, for example, perceive involvement in education as a middle-class, feminine and therefore low-status activity (McGivney, 1998a). Consequently, some feel that participating would entail the risk of exposing themselves to ridicule and losing face. Collective approaches to such groups can help to remove the risk of losing peer respect and acceptance. Workplace initiatives such as the Return-to-Learn programme offered by the public sector trade union UNISON, and employee development schemes which are open to all workers irrespective of their occupational position, have been successful in bringing into education and training many individuals from lower participating groups, including unskilled, semi-skilled, part-time and shift workers. The knowledge that co-workers are participating in learning helps to overcome suspicion or apprehension and often motivates others to do the same.

Different groups inevitably require different approaches and outside the workplace it has been found easier to target some groups than others. Women, for example, are easier to contact than men as they tend to form mutual support networks often around children attending crèches, playgroups or schools.

The role of other people in influencing decisions to participate

The key role that 'other people' play in influencing group or individual decisions to participate in any kind of learning is another consistent finding from practice and research. Babchuk and Courtney (1995) found that these can be either primary 'influentials' as mentioned above (family, friends, co-workers, others in circle), or secondary 'influentials' such as educators, community organisers or employers.

Recent research has confirmed that people are more likely to seek information and advice from known and trusted persons when making decisions about engaging in learning than from official sources of information such as careers and guidance services. Focus groups conducted in London (Archer and Ross, 2001) and in Worcestershire (Dinsdale, 2001) revealed that the most common source of information about learning opportunities was not printed publicity materials but friends, other family members, co-workers or people working closely with the community:

> *Many respondents valued advice and encouragement from family and friends when making decisions about education, but distrusted and felt alienated from official sources of information including careers services. For these people, 'top-down' messages do not work.* (Archer and Ross, 2001)

> *The important element was that they trusted people who they felt knew something about them and the course: 'X felt it was a good course and I would get something from it'.* (Dinsdale, 2001: 3)

Dinsdale's research showed that even those who are ready and prepared to engage in organised learning often need input from other people, in addition to printed information, in order to take the necessary action. Those who said they would seek information from formal sources such as colleges and prospectuses were unlikely to have ever done so:

> *Where people had picked up flyers in the centres or libraries they wanted more information face to face and this was usually about reassurance that the course was suitable for them. Printed material could never give this type of assurance and many said they would not feel confident to ring the number printed on the flyer or go along to a*

session offering advice. The fact that they could talk to others about the course and maybe talk to a friend into coming to the course was important. "1 came because X was coming" was a common comment.

The reassurance sought by word of mouth is a vital stage in ensuring successful, sustainable recruitment and progression. The information wanted is usually around support issues (...) One quote summed it up, 'you need someone to talk to without committing yourself'. The point was made that people were put off by the word 'interview' and being invited in 'for a chat' about the course sounded friendlier. (Dinsdale, 2001: 3 and 14)

This highlights the importance of informal outreach services that provide educational information and advice on a one-to-one basis. Many informants have made the point that guidance located in or connected to Careers Services does not reach those who could most benefit from it.

My study of informal learning (McGivney, 1999a) also revealed that the most important factor in encouraging people who rarely engage in formal learning to participate is the influence of 'key' persons who inform, encourage, advise and support individuals and groups and act as intermediaries between them and education providers. In the examples cited in that study, the 'key' persons included outreach development or guidance workers, health visitors, community leaders, playgroup leaders, head teachers, local 'opinion leaders', union representatives, co-workers and friends. In all the case studies I cited, groups and individuals had become involved in both informal and formal learning activities primarily as a result of the encouragement and support of people such as these. In one case I was told that the key person who disseminated information about workplace learning opportunities and encouraged people to participate was the office cleaner whom everybody knew and respected.

The study on community attitudes to learning (Bowman *et al*, 2000) similarly found that the encouragement and support of a familiar and trusted person often leads individuals who would not otherwise take advantage of education opportunities to engage in learning.

Face-to-face interventions

For those who would never consider engaging in organised learning, therefore – those who perceive it as impossible, undesirable or completely outside their cultural frame of reference – the importance of face-to-face interventions by a trusted individual cannot be under-estimated:

There's no substitute for talking to people.

You've got to spend time on the pre-figurative stuff in the community, talking to people. But no-one sees this as real work. It's too loose and unstructured, but you can't reach these people any other way.

The important thing is the first hook. Once you've got them through the door the possibilities are endless. It's the investment in that stage which is the most important. (Practitioners quoted in McGivney, 1999a)

The most effective recruitment strategies therefore go well beyond the marketing of existing provision or the shifting of pre-determined programmes to an outreach location. They also go beyond simply asking people what kinds of learning programmes they want, as responses to this question are often based on what people think learning means and what they think is available, rather than on their own preferences: 'People don't know what to ask for. You have to talk it through with people to tease out what they need' (Informant). They involve a participatory and interactive process – active involvement with people; listening to their views, concerns and preferences; identifying any learning interests or needs that arise, and responding constructively to them. People who traditionally do not engage in organised learning are far more likely to do so when they are given the opportunity to decide what is of value and relevance to them than when they are offered predetermined, pre-packaged programmes. This is something that past studies have repeatedly shown and which has been confirmed in recent research:

Consultation and negotiation with non-participants on learning needs, curricula, methods of delivery, modes of attendance and styles of learning emerged as key processes in work with new groups. (McGivney, 1990: 177)

Starting from the students' current position and building on their interests, were important features of {interviewees'} experiences and desires. (Bowman et al, 2000: 42)

Constructive listening – listening to what people have to say and what their interests, problems and priorities are before offering any solutions – has been a strong feature of the most effective widening participation schemes (McGivney, 2000). Some recent initiatives have involved provision of educational information and guidance in local health practices, as a result of which some people have taken their first steps back into education since leaving school (McGivney, 1997; James, 2001).

Knowing that their views will be respected and acted upon makes a real difference to people's willingness to engage in learning (Taylor S, 2000). This has been understood by organisations and institutions such as the WEA and some residential colleges which have a good record of working with excluded groups and communities. Other providers have also begun to pursue this strategy. A few years ago Islington Council held a 'Citizens' Conference' as part of a community-led approach to planning and policy development. The opinions and preferences of local people were sought in focus groups and a conference and the findings helped to inform the local adult learning plan. This example fulfils Ryan's (2000) call for:

> *forums where all of the stakeholders, particularly those who are not well served at present, can voice their dissatisfaction and play an active part in refashioning the provision of educational services and the allocation of resources within the services, so that diversity can be nurtured as a source of strength. Forums of this nature are needed at the levels of policy-making and co-ordination of provision as well as at the level of implementation.* (p47)

Offering communities the opportunity to contribute to decisions about the kind of provision available is therefore an effective means of encouraging them to engage in learning:

> *Bringing about a change in culture to create a learning society is not about telling people that learning is good for them; it's about making sure that learning really is good for them. It's about learners and communities playing an active role in determining what is of value and benefit to them.* (Stott, 2001: 18)

Not surprisingly, the spate of recent studies focusing on social exclusion and neighbourhood renewal has come to the same conclusion. The OECD (1999) report on overcoming exclusion stressed the importance of allowing people to define and develop their own learning interests. Similarly, a succession of reports for the British Government (eg. DfEE, 1999b) has argued that people who have had poor school experiences and who find dedicated education centres and institutions remote and intimidating will only take advantage of learning opportunities when these are locally-based and of immediate relevance to their lives and concerns (something which any good community educator could have told policy-makers for nothing!).

Provision of local and relevant community-inspired learning activities has subsequently become a strong theme in current policy:

> *{The Fund} will support activities that will take learning into new sectors of the community not reached by traditional education organisations, providing opportunities that are relevant to the people involved and delivering them in ways that will interest and attract the people who are hardest to reach.* (DfEE, 1998b)

> *Much more of the right kind of learning will be available in ways that meet the needs of local people, on their own terms and in settings with which they are comfortable.* (DfEE: 1999c)

Local learning is a vital part of government plans. Community-based learning has a key role in improving basic skills; providing family learning opportunities, increasing access to FE and HE and increasing opportunities for individuals. (Malcolm Wicks, former Under-Secretary of State for Lifelong Learning[1])

The Government's Neighbourhood Renewal Strategy has also stressed the importance of encouraging local communities to have a say in the planning and management of local services.

After more than a decade of decline, therefore, there has been a sharp increase in community-based learning activities, encouraged by new funding initiatives aimed at contributing to government agendas of lifelong learning, neighbourhood renewal and social inclusion. For these to result in wider participation, however, providers have to take risks and be prepared to invest in the necessary outreach work. This means appointing people with the right blend of skills and ensuring that outreach is a central rather than peripheral activity.

Practice has repeatedly shown that investing in people with local contacts and the necessary networking and communication skills is one of the most effective ways of bringing new groups into learning. In many institutions, however, outreach development workers are on part-time and fractional contracts which inevitably limits the amount they can achieve. Providers who invest in permanent outreach staff and ensure that their pay and conditions are on a par with those of institution-based staff are more likely to succeed in engaging new groups of learners than those who appoint such workers on a year-to-year or project basis. One of the conclusions of *Recovering Outreach* (McGivney, 2000a) was that outreach work should be complementary to, and have parity of esteem with, the mainstream work of an institution.

Outreach skills

Face-to-face work in the community is labour-intensive and time-consuming and demands a diversity of skills:

You have to work very hard to generate the sorts of activities that will attract those groups and not everyone can do it. Some staff don't know what you're talking about. They think it's about advertising. But it' s about completely redesigning and rethinking what you're offering. There are only a small number of people who can do it and they have to be given their head and the resources. It's about identifying key people who can actually make it happen. Some people here wouldn't begin to understand because they were recruited to do a totally different activity. (Interviewee)

---

1 Plenary address at NIACE conference *Funding Adult Learning*, 2 February 2000.

One of the main skills required of those working in the community, especially when targeting the most disadvantaged groups, is the ability to gain the co-operation and trust of the 'gatekeepers' – the people who are most in contact with those communities. In the widening participation partnership work conducted in Oxfordshire (outlined in McGivney, 2000b) development workers succeeded in reaching specific target groups (Asian men, people on probation and in bail hostels, workers in care homes, the homeless and residents in rural communities) only after careful negotiation with individuals such as community and religious leaders, head teachers, employers, bail hostel wardens and probation officers.

Negotiating with the gatekeepers is one of the most important aspects of community-based work as the success of any initiative depends on their co-operation, commitment and support. These can only be gained if they are persuaded of the value of the work to the target groups and assured that there will be no disbenefits to them. Some outreach and development workers have found that gaining the co-operation of community gatekeepers is often more difficult than persuading target groups to participate. Efforts to contact particular groups can be seen as encroachments on individual territory and therefore resisted. Some people do not perceive educational approaches as useful or necessary to the group in question. Others may be over-protective towards the people in their charge or feel threatened by the idea of having better-educated individuals working for or with them. Those who agree to co-operate sometimes have a perception of a group's learning interests and needs that is based more on their own values and beliefs than on those of the group in question.

Approaches to gatekeepers need therefore to be at least as careful and sensitive as those to target groups and this requires experience and skill.

Peer support and role models

Since institutional outreach workers cannot remain indefinitely in the same areas and work exclusively with the same communities, an effective way of sustaining contact and enabling the widening participation work to continue is to train local people in outreach, networking and guidance skills.

> *It may be that the money {for outreach} is best spent supporting the community structures that already exist and identifying 'education champions' from within the community rather than appointing new workers who will spend a good deal of time getting to know the area and gaining the trust of the community before work can begin.* (Dinsdale, 2001: 12)

Use of peer groups to provide encouragement and support to potential or new learners is far more common now than it was a decade ago and there is now a number of schemes that involve training local people to be 'learning champions', 'ambassadors' or guidance 'signposters', or to conduct participatory research into attitudes and learning interests in their own communities.

Training local people as guidance workers was a feature of several DfEE-funded demonstration outreach projects (Watson and Tyers, 1998), and there are now several other examples throughout the country. One is a scheme linked to the Bolton Information Network which involves training local people in outreach work, communication skills, advice and guidance, working with others and basic skills awareness. The resulting team of community learning ambassadors has had some success in attracting different groups into learning, supporting learners and helping them to progress in a number of ways. According to a member of the team, they are able to disseminate information about local learning opportunities far more effectively than other sources and, as they are known and trusted in the community, people act on the information:

> *In a few weeks we had a waiting list. Who better to approach than someone who's been there, done that worn the Tee shirt and is still wearing it with enjoyment?* [2]

Local learning ambassadors (or whatever else they are called) who have themselves been actively involved in learning, act as role models in their communities and encourage others to follow their example. This has been understood by the TUC which, with support from the Union Learning Fund, has trained over 2,000 lay 'Learning Representatives' to take on a front-line role in workplaces.

FEFC (2000a) found that peer group role models also contribute to successful learning. The report highlights measures such as inviting former students from similar backgrounds to help during induction or in the early stages of learning; establishing mentoring or 'study-buddy' systems and taking advantage of national initiatives to promote the idea that people from the same background can succeed.

The most popular recommendation arising from The Islington Citizens' Conference, held to consult local people on the content of the Adult Learning Plan, was for the setting up of 'handholding' or mentoring services that would advise and support new learners before, during and after courses and in taking their next steps (Jude, 2001).

Tutors

The importance of 'other' people to successful participation continues throughout the learning situation: 'It's the people (tutors) who make a difference and if you take

---

them out of the equation you won't get the results' (Informant).

Like outreach workers, tutors need particular skills in working with new adult learners as they are often required to perform multiple roles such as:

> *informal counsellors, social workers, support workers, careers advisers, administrators and facilitators as well as teachers. In a sense the learning experience (...) is more challenging than on a mainstream course in that the learner has more autonomy and therefore more responsibility.* (Grennan, 2000: 32)

It has also been found that being taught by people with similar characteristics (such as gender, race, cultural background) can be a great motivator among the most excluded groups (Social Care Research, 1998).

Responding to identified interests

People, therefore, are the most important element in any widening participation strategy, but it is how providers respond to the learning interests that are identified that will result in actual engagement.

Analysts often make a distinction between 'intrinsic' motivation to learn – learning because of an inner drive or desire to succeed or out of curiosity or interest, and 'extrinsic' motivation – learning for instrumental or social reasons or because it is a requirement, for example, of the job.

The main expressed purposes for entering post-compulsory education and training have not changed much over the years, with most people tending to cite extrinsic goals related to work, personal development and educational progression albeit with some differences between groups and cohorts. The NIACE 1996 survey (Sargant *et al*, 1997) showed that adults from the lower socio-economic groups were more likely than those from the higher ones to cite instrumental reasons for learning; older learners and women were likely to be learning for personal development and interest; while men were more likely to be involved for employment-related reasons. Nevertheless, 71 per cent of the current and recent learners who responded to that survey said they were learning to improve their working position – a situation that has changed little in subsequent surveys.

People who have not engaged in any organised learning since leaving school often say that they might do so if they judged it to be immediately 'useful'. Perceptions of usefulness usually relate to acquisition of employment or changes in employment (which in part explains the widespread popularity of learning to use computers as a first subject choice). For many people undertaking learning primarily for work reasons, the link between learning and jobs needs to be explicit and wherever possible, linked with the actual labour market (McGivney, 1992b). There are some good examples of this. *Catering for Jobs* is a programme that has been running in Croydon for over five years. Funded by the local authority, ESF and the former TEC, it is targeted at single parents who have never had a job living on the New Addington Estate. The programme is free and runs in a school domestic science suite. Help with childcare is provided and all materials are free. Many participants get jobs or progress into other college courses:

> *The books were link with jobs and something they felt they could do, To some adult educators the idea of learning for work is anathema but if you speak to participants it's extremely important.* (Interviewee)

One has to be cautious, however, in taking expressed motivations to learn totally at face value as it is often found that once people actually engage in learning, they begin to express more intrinsic reasons. To take just one example, in a survey of participants in the Unison Return-to-Learn programme,

> *only 10 per cent identified their main motive as immediately job-related while a staggering 72 per cent had motives like 'get back into education', 'gain confidence', 'show myself I still had a brain'.* (Uden, 1996: 37)

Indirect routes into learning

Moreover, a large number of people re-enter structured and organised learning for reasons unrelated to any specifically defined learning goals. Adult routes back into learning are not always direct. My own work has frequently shown that, for many people, the first steps back are often accidental and unplanned – because others are doing it; because they have become involved in issues of local interest or concern; because they want to help their children succeed at school, or because learning opportunities have been made available in a place they frequent for another purpose.

Although none of these situations originates in a specific desire to learn, each of them can lead to engagement in learning and the acquisition of a taste for learning. All therefore present opportunities to widen participation by such means as group targeting, responding to community priorities and interests, setting up family learning schemes, or providing informal learning opportunities in premises established for another purpose.

Informal learning starting points

There is evidence that it is often through informal – and unrecognised – learning that people embark on a more structured learning trajectory. This often starts with involvement in groups and activities that are not immediately concerned or associated with learning. Studies (for example, Percy *et al*, 1988; Elsdon *et al*, 1995; Foley, 1999) have shown that the learning that flows from membership of voluntary organisations, from social action and protest, or from engagement in a collective concern or enterprise, can significantly increase individual and group confidence levels, lead to the acquisition of a range of practical skills and stimulate new interests that often lead people into structured learning.

In my research into the role of pre-schools in creating learning opportunities for adults (McGivney, 1998b), I found that many of the parents and carers who were actively involved in the running and administration of the groups were undertaking a significant amount of learning – about children, their development and how they learn; about holding and chairing meetings; about budgeting and fundraising, staffing issues, health and safety and child protection matters. None of the parents or carers interviewed described this process as 'learning' although it was learning of an extraordinarily rich, dynamic and transformative kind which had led many of them into formal education, into employment and into other voluntary roles in the community.

As this example demonstrates, women often return to learning via a non-educational route. In a society that places little value on parenting and provides few supports for young mothers, it is often in small community projects, voluntary groups and pre-schools that they find the social contacts, help and support that they need. Many women have become confident and successful learners, found greater personal fulfilment, and gained employment after becoming involved in mother-and-toddler groups, playgroups or centres that offer crèche facilities.

An evaluation study I undertook in Northern Ireland showed this process very clearly. In the 1980s, women without qualifications or jobs living in some of the poorest areas of Belfast came together in community centres because crèches were made available. Collectively, they began to voice concerns about the lack of health facilities and play space for their children and their need to gain the confidence to express their concerns to officials, health professionals and politicians. With the help of community workers and educational development workers from the Women's Education Project – a tiny organisation funded almost entirely from charitable sources – they explored ways of making positive collective and individual changes. The initial group discussions gradually evolved into more structured learning courses – creative writing, assertiveness, group-building skills – that responded to emerging interests and concerns. The outcomes for both groups and individuals were astounding. By 1990, some groups had written their own constitution and were running themselves and some had conducted research into local living conditions and presented their findings to politicians. Many individual women in the groups visited had moved from a situation of isolation to one of active involvement in the community. Some had gained the confidence to seek jobs, to take on other community roles and to enrol in local college courses. Some had trained as tutors and were now running adult education courses themselves (McGivney, 1991).

Active involvement in local issues or concerns frequently generates learning. In my study of informal learning (McGivney, 1999a) I cited the example of a large estate in Leicester where local residents had become worried about the impact on them of a proposed building development. They asked a community education worker for advice and with his help embarked on a collective process of learning about planning applications, how to register opposition and how to communicate with officials. The group met regularly to explore these issues with contributions from local politicians and representatives from the local authority and other relevant agencies According to the community education worker: 'a whole host of learning opportunities spiralled out of those initial pragmatic goals'. As the group's interests broadened, they began to conduct local research and, eventually, became involved in writing a book about the history of the estate.

In this case, several factors stimulated the initial learning process, which illustrates the importance of the points made earlier in this chapter: it arose out of identified needs and concerns; local people themselves decided what they needed to know, and it was organised in a way that built organically on what was happening in the community.

The same example also showed that, in an informal learning context, the number of actual participants can be a misleading guide to the real impact of learning. Although the learning group numbered about 15, there was, according to the community worker:

> *an active periphery of about 80. The small groups passed on their learning and we got feedback from a much wider group. We were servicing a network rather than a defined group of learners.* (McGivney, 1999a)

Informal learning can therefore be an important means of creating a 'critical mass' of local learners: local people learning together in the community can become a network and a resource for each other.

> *There are a lot of misconceptions about informal learning. A lot of it is collective. It's not just the group that are ostensibly involved. It operates by a cascade process. Information is passed on and cascades out into the community. There are organic networks and if informal learning can tap into these you can achieve far more than with those you meet on*

a regular basis. You can have a major impact in terms of social stability with a piece of learning that involves eight people. The key is to use kinship or wider family networks, and train people to disseminate information in forms that are easily replicable. (Community education worker quoted in McGivney, 1999a)

Despite the differences between groups, locations and activities, the examples mentioned above had certain features in common: in each case the learning arose out of people's immediate lives, priorities and preoccupations and in each case there was a discernible pattern of evolution. As a result of the 'organic' learning generated through the development of interests, community activism or involvement in voluntary groups, people's confidence increased; their interests widened and they eventually identified a desire for more information or new skills. At this stage they were ready to embark upon a more planned and structured learning process although none had initially considered or planned to enter any form of organised learning. As observed by an outreach worker, there comes a point at which 'people see what they are doing as relevant to their interests not education in the abstract. They suddenly see that education can be relevant. This is a huge leap.' (McGivney, 1999a). This is a critical turning point which marks a significant change in educational self-concept for the individuals concerned: they now see themselves as 'learners'.

Collective learning

Once this transition is made there is often a shift from collective learning to an individualised learning process of the kind with which we are all familiar, involving structured taught provision. In the beginning, however, community-based learning is frequently a collective rather than an individual process, motivated by factors such as pursuit of common interests, the need for information on local issues, the desire to solve a local problem, or concerns about health or safety matters, the environment or children's development and welfare. Despite this, current policy still envisages education as a wholly individual process conducted in isolation from the family, social and community contexts in which people lead their lives.

An effective way of involving people in learning of any kind is therefore to tap into their immediate priorities and concerns.

People need to be attracted by alternative learning which supports their own goals or triggers their enthusiasm, creates a positive self-image and enables people better to act in their own interests. (Howard, 2001: 5)

Through my own work I have become increasingly convinced of the value of informal learning both for its own sake and as a means of revitalising communities.

From the point of view of widening participation, however, it also acts as a conduit to more structured learning for many people who would not normally consider undertaking an organised education or training programme.

There is, therefore:

huge potential for stimulating demand {for learning} through unleashing the learning in existing interest groups, membership organisations, social and humanitarian movements and some forms of enterprise. These are nurseries in which more knowledge and skills related learning can be cultivated. (Howard, 2000: 6)

Helping children to learn

Many people who have not engaged in post-compulsory education are nevertheless anxious to help their children to achieve and this often leads them back into learning themselves. In the NIACE 1996 survey, nearly half of those who described themselves as current or recent learners stated that they had wanted to help their children to learn (although the relationship between this desire and their own learning was unexplored).

There are now many examples of family learning schemes in which parents and children learn together and separately in small programmes run in co-operation with local schools. These frequently start adults on a formal learning trajectory. Studies of four family literacy and numeracy pilots supported by the Basic Skills Agency showed that participants' reading and writing skills improved significantly and although many had not studied since leaving school, 70 per cent continued onto a further course (Hemstedt, 2000: 20-21).

Whereas many of the adults involved in family literacy schemes are women, in some areas men have been specifically invited to help children in schools and this has proved an effective means of involving some of the male groups who are among the most difficult to engage in any learning programme (McGivney, 1998a).

Courses for voluntary helpers in schools can also provide a route back into learning. An Open College-accredited course, run by the WEA and funded from a variety of sources, has been targeted at people who left school early with no or few qualifications. The 10-week course involves learning about the workings and curriculum of a primary school and includes a number of practical activities. There is also a voluntary placement in a primary school. After being piloted in 1994, the course is now running in 30 LEAs across the country. By the end of the summer term 1999 it had run 324 times with 3,293 students completing, 82 per cent of whom gained credits. A further 1,300 were expected to complete in the following year. A survey of participants who had completed the course in Yorkshire between 1996 and 1998 showed that 40 per cent had subsequently gained employment as classroom assistants, midday supervisors, playgroup leaders and after-school club workers. Nearly 200 had progressed into other education and training courses ranging from GCSEs to degrees and teacher training courses. Over half of respondents had continued voluntary work in primary schools and 43 had become school governors (*Individual Learning News*, 2000b).

Providing learning activities in places established for other purposes

Local premises that provide learning opportunities in addition to their principal function frequently lead people to engage in structured learning. They come for one thing and stay for another. There are countless examples of how community centres, pre-school playgroups, clubs, pubs and leisure centres, among others, have become important sites of learning in addition to their primary purpose. To give just one example: during my study of informal learning I visited a working men's club in a former mining area. This housed a resource centre which offered advice on welfare matters to local unemployed people as well as a range of informal learning opportunities. Many of the people who had engaged in learning programmes at the centre had originally visited it for another purpose – for social reasons, for advice on welfare rights or for help with job search. Having found the venue welcoming and comfortable, they had returned and had gradually been drawn into the wider range of activities available which included learning to use computers and foreign language classes. None of the learners I spoke to had previously considered approaching an education or training centre. At the time of my visit, two ex-miners were attending teacher-training courses as a direct result of the support and learning activities provided, and a number of regular attenders who had become learners had taken on volunteer roles at the centre (McGivney, 1999a).

This example indicates that offering information and assistance with everyday issues and problems can be an effective first hook. When people feel comfortable and relaxed in a venue, they will often get drawn into the wider range of activities available there. This is an approach that has been successfully used in basic skills provision over the years. Mobile services, for example, have often attracted people back into learning by initially offering assistance with form-filling, health matters or welfare rights. One has effectively used cooking demonstrations as a means of improving numeracy.

Life crises or transitions

In addition to these indirect routes into learning, it is well established that critical life events or adversity frequently act as a motivator or catalyst. As one interviewee claimed: 'Most of my deepest learning experiences have come from crises'. Another observed that some of the most 'inventive' community education has arisen from 'embattled situations' such as the miners' strike in the 1980s.

The NIACE survey undertaken in 1996 (Sargant *et al*, 1997) found that a significant proportion of current or recent learners had recently undergone a life crisis or transition: 59 per cent had recently moved home; 45 per cent had split from their partner; 45 per cent had lost their job; 39 per cent had started a family; 33 per cent had taken early retirement and 32 per cent had had an illness. Although the specific relationship between these life events and decisions to engage in learning was not explored, it is likely that there was some correlation. Other more in-depth studies have found evidence of such a link. Hayes' (1999) study of mature women students in further education, for example, indicated that the need to deal with problems such as poverty, broken relationships, unsupportive partners and other difficult life situations had often started interviewees on a learning trajectory.

Although one cannot, of course, create such situations as a means of prompting learning, the common finding that life crises and turning points often lead people into structured learning programmes suggests that we should not be too disturbed by the large proportion of survey respondents who say that nothing would encourage them to learn.

* * *

The examples outlined above indicate that adults return to learning via a number of different routes and for a wide range of reasons, some of which may, initially, have little to do with specific learning goals or an overt interest in education. This is something that policy with its emphasis on individuals and instrumental objectives continuously fails to take into account. What they collectively demonstrate is that a diversity of activities – informal outreach approaches, using key individuals as change agents, help with everyday problems and issues, discussion groups, family learning initiatives and provision of information or taster courses in places frequented for other purposes – can all help to open a door that many people feel had previously been slammed shut.

> *The initial support offered need not always take the form of classes with paid tutors. People have been attracted back to learning through information and advice on local learning opportunities, access to premises, and use of facilities for meetings and self-generated activities.* (McGivney, 1990: 178)

It is frequently found that, once the first 'hook' has been provided, whatever its form or content, many people subsequently continue learning. This can happen at any stage along the continuum from informal to formal learning. In all the examples mentioned (pre-schools, women's groups in Northern Ireland, the working men's club, the estate in Leicester), a number of individuals who had never previously engaged in post-school education or training eventually moved from informal into organised learning as well as into other socially and personally valuable activities.

Imaginative and responsive programmes for new groups of learners often encourage the development of a learning habit. A survey of participants in UNISON's Return-to-Learn scheme, for example, showed that about 60 per cent of respondents had continued in some form of organised learning (Uden, 1996).

This kind of progression often only happens when people have changed – to borrow the words of Bowman *et al* (2000) – their 'educational self-concept'. Thus a key process in the early stages of any widening participation intervention is to raise people's confidence so that they can see themselves not as educational failures as so many have done in the past, but as successful learners. Raising learner confidence is therefore a critical issue in widening participation.

Another crucial requirement is to offer more than a one-off activity that does not lead anywhere – something that results all too often from the habitual short-term funding of widening participation activities. Focus groups held in Worcestershire (Dinsdale, 2001) revealed that there had been no follow-up to some informal, community-based learning activities: 'There is a feeling of "catching learning" and then being left "high and dry"' (p13). This echoes the findings of a number of studies including *Education's for other People* (McGivney, 1990). Like many other analysts, Dinsdale highlights the need for progression routes, although she stresses that these should not automatically involve moves into formal educational settings. Education providers should 'explore the possibilities of provision of all levels within local venues'.

However desirable this may be, it is not always possible to provide all forms and levels of learning in community settings and this often means that people get involved in a cycle of same level courses rather than moving into more appropriate provision because of their (understandable) attachment to a familiar and comfortable local venue (Bowman *et al*, 2000).

For those who wish or need to make the transition to a formal learning environment, such a move has to be carefully supported or they may be put off education for a second time, and this time for life.

Supporting learners

Flexibility (delivery mechanisms based on recognition of adults' employment and family responsibilities) and *support* are the keys to helping people to achieve a successful transition from informal to more formal learning. Some providers have made tremendous efforts to offer opportunities characterised by both these features. However, although learning institutions are, on the whole, far more flexible than they were a decade ago, many people who move from an informal to a formal learning environment have difficulty adjusting to the loss of the supportive ambience they experienced in an informal local setting. Moreover, they may feel isolated if, because of characteristics such as age, gender, disability, race or the nature of their learning, they are in a minority and if the conditions in which they are expected to learn signal that they are marginal and lower-status students.

Widening participation is not just about access and getting people in; it is also about retention (keeping them going) and achievement (helping them succeed). Support for learners is absolutely vital throughout these stages:

> *Recent debates about increasing participation in HE and opening up access to 'elite' institutions have focused on barriers to entry, but (…) this is only a part of the story. Our case study has pointed to the need to support non-traditional students once they are in HE as well as before they arrive.* (Bamber and Tett, 2001: 15)

A critical factor in engaging new learners and encouraging learning success is therefore provision of support before, throughout and on completion of learning activity: 'if you don't have support mechanisms running through all widening participation interventions you won't widen participation' (Interviewee).

These should involve both practical support and learning support. The most common forms of practical support – financial help, provision of transport; help with childcare, facilities for people with disabilities, provision of refreshments or meals (e.g. for homeless people) – have all helped under-represented groups of learners to participate successfully in organised learning programmes. Practical support can also involve relatively simple things such as sensitive use of language (terms like 'basic education' and 'guidance' can put people off as they suggest a deficiency); reductions in enrolment queues and form-filling; and attention to the composition of staffing with respect to its gender and racial composition.

Learning support, as discussed in *Opening Colleges to Adult Learners* and *Staying or Leaving the Course* (McGivney, 1992a and 1996), can take different forms ranging from ongoing guidance and assistance with basic literacy and numeracy skills and ESOL to use of open learning or ICT materials to support curriculum delivery and learning. Other frequently identified support measures are itemised in the FEFC good practice guide (1997) and FEFC report on widening participation and raising standards (2000a). These include flexible entry points; initial guidance and assessment; strategies to identify and support learners at risk of underachieving; tutorial arrangements that include part-time students and those in community-based provision; assistance with transition to main college sites; support for learners with specific learning difficulties and/or disabilities; access to welfare advice and personal counselling (including advice on financial matters); teaching materials which include positive images of people from different backgrounds; prompt feedback and recognition of achievements and support with progression to other learning.

The FEFC *Guide to Good Practice* (1997) stresses that support, and information about its availability, should be given to all learners *including* (my emphasis) those in outreach centres. The guide also suggests that learners should be actively involved in planning how they are supported and that support should be tailored to meet individual learner needs.

A number of studies cited in *Staying or Leaving the Course* (McGivney, 1996) have indicated that successful learning and completion of programmes are dependent on the extent to which learners feel environmentally, socially and academically 'integrated' in a learning environment. This implies the need to offer support in all these spheres. Non-traditional learners will not feel at ease in a learning environment if they are physically separated from its main buildings or campuses as this can reinforce their actual or perceived marginality. As FEFC (2000a) stresses, new learners need higher rather than lower quality accommodation and learning conditions – a point that is often made by those concerned with widening participation:

> *It's important to provide new groups with higher quality in terms of tutors, premises etc – than anyone else. Arguably, A-level students need less in terms of quality support. We need the best facilities for these groups.* (Interviewee)

To assist social integration, some institutions provide social spaces where new learner groups can meet for mutual networking and support. As has been found in the NIACE research on work with groups with learning difficulties (*Social Care Research*, 1998), learners from marginalised groups need to have a sense of belonging in order to succeed.

A relevant curriculum

Academic integration involves offering people a curriculum that is culturally, socially and personally relevant to them. This can be achieved by negotiating some or all of the content with them and by not being over-prescriptive. Many providers have succeeded in bringing in a broader mix of learners by providing courses tailored specifically to the requirements of groups such as people who are unemployed, those with few or no qualifications, ethnic minority communities, single parents, young people excluded from school, people with special learning needs or disabilities and homeless people. However, the fact that these programmes have so often been financed not by mainstream funding but by short-term finance from sources such as the European Social Fund, the Single Regeneration Budget or the Adult and Community Learning Fund has always ensured that they are of lower importance and status than mainstream programmes.

Policy-makers tend to draw a distinction for funding purposes between vocational and certificated (high status) programmes and non-vocational and non-accredited (low status) programmes whereas, as argued above, adults have very diverse reasons for undertaking education and training and can enrol in a course for a combination of social, instrumental and self-development motives:

> *Too often we prescribe the boundaries of the learning on offer too narrowly. As one student in a literacy class for adults with learning difficulties told a colleague a decade ago, 'I want to learn about Jesus and history, and thunder and lightning.'* (Tuckett, 2001a)

Moreover, as Mayo and Collymore (2000) point out, it is possible to design courses which combine both liberal education values and instrumental objectives:

> *There is no inherent reason why people should not have economic as well as social, cultural and political goals just as they may combine individual with collective aspirations. Individuals may and do aim to improve their employability through learning while sharing group aspirations for collective community benefits.* (p144)

They cite as an example *Action learning in the Community* (ALIC), the result of collaboration between Goldsmiths and Lewisham Colleges and Community Education. The programme combines learning for employability with learning for active citizenship and democracy, and builds on experiential learning in the community to promote successful outcomes both for individuals and for groups.

The question of accreditation inevitably arises in any consideration of provision for new adult learners. As argued in Chapter 4, pressure in the form of assessment and accreditation can deter people in the first instance and FEFC (2000a) acknowledges that non-threatening methods of assessment are essential to recruiting and retaining learners from under-represented groups. Many individuals, however, may eventually be prepared to progress to accredited courses (Grennan, 2000), and practitioners have found that when introduced sensitively and gradually, appropriate accreditation can increase learner confidence and sense of achievement:

> *You need appropriate accreditation to meet learners' needs. I think we need to design carefully so that 'assessment' isn't a bugbear but goes with the spirit of the course.*

Accreditation can give immense pleasure as well as progression power to learners. (Interviewee)

The Open College Networks (OCNs) have demonstrated that programmes which include optional accreditation are popular with new learners and encourage them to achieve, a lesson that recently has been taken on board in UfI (learndirect) courses:

Learners, particularly those who have not received any formal recognition of their achievements in the past, value the way the OCN Credit Record gives recognition to each 'small step' or unit of their learning. It boosts their confidence, makes them feel proud of their achievements and often helps to spur them onto study further to accumulate more credits. (FEFC, 2000a: 29)

Recognising the diverse benefits of learning

As stressed by the FEFC (2000a), widening participation involves making sure that people become successful learners and subsequently progress in whatever direction they choose. It is important, therefore, to recognise the benefits of learning that are valued by learners, as well as those valued by policy-makers and funders.

My research into the factors affecting successful outcomes of foundation training in Coventry (McGivney and Thomson, 1995) revealed that many unemployed and disadvantaged individuals identified the greatest benefits as something other than the acquisition of certificates, occupationally-specific skills and jobs. Despite the wide diversity of organisations, target groups and training programmes, the testimony of learners was strikingly similar. Virtually all the current and former students interviewed identified the major benefit derived from participation as significantly increased confidence. Associated gains such as increased assertiveness skills, enhanced self-esteem and greater independence were also frequently mentioned, especially by women, a number of whom commented that participation had proved to them (and their families) that they were capable of being more than wives and mothers. Many perceived this change in self-perception and others' perceptions of them as far more important than practical or technical skills. Interviewees also reported that the increased confidence gained through participation was a key factor in motivating them to enrol in other training and education courses, to seek employment and to apply for a wider range of jobs.

Whole-institution strategies

It is clear from existing practice that there has to be total commitment to widening participation from institutional management and an approach that involves the whole institution:

> *We beavered away in ILEA but unless we got our hands on real power we didn't make much difference. Then we became managers and started changing things. But then came Thatcherism and cuts.* (Interviewee)

> *I think it's absolutely critical that you have a whole institution approach that actually spells out that this {WP} direction is a priority otherwise you simply get more of the same.* (Interviewee)

According to the FEFC *Guide to Good Practice* (1997), the colleges which have achieved most in widening participation have had the support and commitment of governors, management and staff, and have underpinned their commitment to the process with strategic objectives, operational plans, funding strategies and quality assurance arrangements which include staff development and student tracking. Many have also entered into partnership arrangements with other providers and agencies to develop new learning opportunities for excluded groups:

> *Partnerships can bring value added: they're important from a bidding point of view and good from a synergy and resource point of view (you can do more together than apart).* (Forrester and Payne, 1999)

National campaigns

Education and training providers on their own, however, can only achieve limited local changes in adult participation patterns. To achieve change at a national level will require a significant cultural shift. This will not happen overnight, although national policy measures and campaigns can help to change attitudes and perceptions.

Sargant and Tuckett (1997) argue that mass campaigns can change cultures of participation and achievement, as happened with the national adult literacy movement of the 1970s which successfully combined media and outreach activities.

The annual Adult Learners' Week, which also involves media promotion, local initiatives and targeted activities, has also helped to change perceptions and prompted new people to participate.

> *The Week has taught us a lot about how to promote the value of learning to those least susceptible to its charms.* (Interviewee)

{It} has had a huge impact and has brought about a huge change in understanding of what it meant by adult learning. The awards have had a very important impact locally. If you line up award winners (they're usually widening participation students) in front of VIPs, it changes people's perceptions about who does it. (Yarnit, 2000: 23)

Targeted activities associated with the Week have included putting details of the information and advice helpline with the Giro cheques sent to people claiming unemployment benefit (Job Seekers' Allowance) during the two weeks leading up to the Week. This has led to a large increase in the number of callers who are registered unemployed.

Use of TV has also had a considerable impact. Sargant and Tuckett (1997) point out that because of its universal reach, TV provides the cheapest method of mass delivery to people in their own homes. The use of short promotional films during Adult Learners' Week has provided valuable role models and made people aware of the learndirect information and advice Helpline. Follow-up surveys after the Week in 1999 and 2000 showed that the majority of callers, especially women and older adults, had been made aware of the service through TV. In 1999, over 70 per cent of callers took action after calling it. The effectiveness of TV in prompting learning has also been demonstrated by BBC Education campaigns such as *Computers don't bite* and *Webwise*, and *Brookie Basics* on Channel 4.

* * *

Existing practice over the last three decades shows that there is a wide range of approaches through which excluded groups can be drawn into structured learning and supported through the learning process. To what extent does current policy encourage and support these?

Chapter 7

The impact of current policy

Since the election of the Labour Government in May 1997 there has been a rapid succession of developments and initiatives in post-compulsory learning, many of which have had the explicit aim of increasing demand for structured learning among the groups most resistant to it.

In contrast to the early 1990s, there has been a stress on the wider aims and benefits of learning, particularly the contribution adult and community learning can make to reducing poverty and regenerating deprived neighbourhoods. As David Blunkett, former Secretary of State for Education and Employment, said in the Learning and Skills Council remit letter dated 9 November 2000, 'We must ensure that lifelong learning becomes a battering ram against exclusion as well as a motor for economic regeneration.'

Policy Action Team reports for the Social Exclusion Unit have suggested that past approaches have been too top-down and short-term and that in order to achieve community renewal there is a need to recognise the problems people face and take account of local as well as government concerns and priorities. Listening to learners and potential learners has therefore become an important dimension of policy: 'We must place the learner at the heart of the new system' (DfEE, 1999a). The Learning and Skills Council is accordingly expected to be driven by identified learning needs rather than 'central design or existing routes'. It has a duty to promote and increase demand for learning and to secure 'a step change' in national learning and skills performance.

There is an acceptance at policy level that useful learning can take place not only in dedicated educational environments and the workplace but also in diverse sites including the home and the community. *Learning to Succeed* (DfEE, 1999a), the White Paper which preceded the Learning and Skills Act of 2000, recognised the unsuitability of formal delivery for many people and the need for flexible and responsive local learning opportunities. Among the principles espoused in the White Paper, several were explicitly related to widening participation – investing in learning to benefit everyone, removing the barriers to learning and putting people first.

A number of steps have already been taken to achieve these aims including the establishment of strategic learning partnerships across England, generous increases in funding for adult learning, and the introduction of two new funding streams – the Union Learning Fund and the Adult and Community Learning Fund. Other initiatives intended to have an impact on adult participation patterns are:

- postcode premiums in further and higher education
- the introduction of Individual Learning Accounts (ILAs) and the University for industry (UfI)
- the establishment of learndirect centres and UK Online
- finance for Information Advice and Guidance (IAG) partnerships and the national lifelong learning helpline
- the launch of a national adult literacy and numeracy skills strategy
- the introduction of the Special Educational Needs and Disability Bill
- the piloting of educational maintenance allowances for young people staying on in education, and
- a range of funding measures designed to assist communities including a Community Group ILA pilot which aims to reach people in deprived areas by working with credit unions and local schools and targeting both lone parents and carers.

The new structure for post-16 education has been given a strong remit for increasing and widening adult participation. The funding formula of the Learning and Skills Council recognises disadvantage and additional needs and allows for free provision for people on benefit and their dependants. The 47 Local Learning and Skills Councils are required to give a high priority to meeting the learning needs of socially disadvantaged groups and deprived communities, and to ensure that a wide range of learning opportunities is available. They can also support innovative local work with flexible discretionary funds.

Recently the LSC has launched a nationwide 'Bite-Size' course campaign to give people without experience of post-16 education a taste for learning.

In higher education, the least equitable sector in terms of student intake, there has also been a series of moves to widen participation – premiums for attracting certain categories of students; funding for wider participation initiatives; fee waivers and loans for some part-time students; an extension of the Disabled Students' Allowances to part-time and postgraduate students; the *Excellence in Cities* initiative to encourage greater links with schools; and the introduction of bursaries and other kinds of help for low-income and mature students. In addition, benchmark indicators have been introduced to measure individual institutions' progress in redressing the under-representation of certain social groups.

Thus there has been a multi-stranded approach to widening participation and some very positive changes. Among these one can highlight as particularly significant the long-overdue ending of the Schedule 2/Non-Schedule 2 curriculum divide; financial incentives to increase adult learning opportunities and people's access to them, and measures to give local people a greater say in determining the kind of opportunities that are provided. There is, therefore, some optimism about the general direction of policy as the comments from three of the people interviewed suggest:

Things are getting much less worse. There are enough measures to make us feel really cheerful.

At least widening participation is now centre stage. It is a historical moment. We are at a unique point in time. Because we've had almost 20 years without policy we had little practice.

The really encouraging thing about all this stuff is a massive faith in people taking on their own learning agenda.

One of the biggest differences since the 1990s is that whereas the access movement originated in practice, current moves to widen participation have been policy-led. They have been top-down rather than bottom-up, with the government taking an unprecedented lead although, as pointed out by Stuart (2000), the underlying aims are not necessarily the same as those of the social purpose developments of 30 years ago: 'It would be foolish to assume that there is a necessary connection between older notions of a social purpose, popular or radical education and the widening participation agenda' (p23).

Many of the new strategies are beginning to pay off. Learning opportunities in the community and in the workplace have increased: 'One of the most exciting things is the way the unions have taken up learning in recent years, The Union Learning Fund is having a real effect' (Interviewee).

ILAs have already exceeded the target of a million accounts opened by 2002 and, despite accusations of provider malpractice and their subsequent suspension, there is some evidence that they have helped people who would not otherwise have been able or willing to pay for learning (Payne, 2000).

The Learndirect Helpline, which was launched in 1998, had received 2.5 million calls by May 2000 and by the same period, UfI had 70 learning hubs, over 1,000 learning centres, and had attracted 100,000 learners.

Staying-on rates have increased by up to 10 per cent in areas where education maintenance allowances are being piloted, and their impact has apparently been especially positive on boys and young people from poorer backgrounds (Piatt, 2001).

Government measures have also had an impact on providers. There now seems to be a shared agenda for change in all sectors, as well as greater awareness and understanding of participation issues and how institutions themselves often construct barriers. FEFC reports (2000a and b) comment on the substantial progress the further education sector has made since 1997 in recruiting learners from disadvantaged backgrounds and in raising standards. The reports found that widening participation is now a core part of most college strategic plans and objectives and that colleges have adopted a more systematic, institution-wide approach to widening participation. In many it is now a mainstream rather than marginal concern overseen by a designated senior manager.

Positive changes have also occurred in some higher education institutions:

Suddenly these things – widening participation and support have become very important and these changes have consequences in the way in which this university sees itself and presents and promotes itself, and in the way it operates in terms of promotion procedures, etc. There's much more stress on retention now and this is having an impact. This means learner and learning support are now being re-positioned within the university. Before the staff working in these areas were not seen as making a contribution to the 'real' business of the university. They're now seen as very important. (Interviewee)

Back in the 80s there was very little serious monitoring going on around widening participation. Now at least we know who we're reaching in terms of equal opportunity issues. Monitoring, target-setting and record keeping are very helpful. They concentrate people's minds and lead to development of strategies. They have shown us how serious the problems are in terms of socio-economic groups. (Interviewee)

Some have also found that local authority adult education services have acquired greater importance and status:

The Adult Education service now has greater credibility. The acceptance that accessible opportunities should be available has impacted not just on FEFC-funded provision but also on LEA provision. Now it's not something you're slightly ashamed of being part of. (Interviewee)

Publicly-funded providers and institutions are more prepared than a decade ago to work together and most are now involved in a range of partnerships with other organisations and institutions (albeit in some cases to achieve funding or target numbers rather than to achieve a more accessible and equitable system):

As a result of the participation rates[1] Government has set, HEIs will be forced to work together otherwise they'll all be fishing in the same pond. We can only achieve a 50 per cent participation rate through collaboration between HEIs, schools, FE, employers and other sectors. (Interviewee)

---

1 Higher education institutions were told in 1998 to recruit an extra 100,000 students between 1998-99 and 2001-02. Much of the expansion was expected to be at sub-degree level in colleges.

At face value, therefore, these developments suggest that the 'step change' in adult participation envisaged by ministers may be well on the way to being achieved. Unfortunately, however, there are certain contradictions in policy that may make it difficult to produce any significant overall change in adult participation patterns.

Continuing political emphasis on younger learners

The emphasis in current policy is still predominantly on younger learners in spite of ministerial commitment to 'lifelong' learning and the fact that the majority of learners in post-compulsory education are over 19. (In 1998-1999, less than 20 per cent of students taking FEFC-funded courses were under 19.) As Alan Tuckett (2001b) has observed, 'the new law still gives young learners entitlements and adults get what is left over'.

In the LSC corporate plan, the only planned new participation target related to the 16-18 cohort, and expenditure was skewed in their favour. According to one report (*Working Brief*, 2001b(a)), the announced budget rise to support increased participation in further education was worth twice as much for 16-18-year-olds as for those aged over 19, regardless of regional disparities in staying-on rates and achievement levels among the different age cohorts. Similarly, student support arrangements in the new structures privilege full-time study taken mainly by younger adults over part-time study undertaken primarily by older adults.

This has caused dismay among those concerned with increasing opportunities for adult learners:

> *Much of the government's ring-fenced funding for further education will benefit less than a fifth of further education students. Millions of extra pounds are being poured into colleges to recruit more 16-18-year-olds but more than 80 per cent of students are adults, most studying part-time.* (Tysome, 2000a)

As in the past when local authorities were expected to make 'adequate' provision for adults, policy, as expressed in the 2000 Learning and Skills Act, is still extremely vague about the nature and scale of learning opportunities for adults that will be provided by the learning and skills councils:

> *At the end of two years' hard debate on the importance of community learning, the Learning and Skills Act offered just this to adult learners, 'The (Learning and Skills) Council must secure the provision of reasonable facilities' for post-19 education'. And what is reasonable? 'Facilities are reasonable if...the facilities are of such a quantity and quality that the Council can reasonably be expected to secure their provision.'* (Tuckett, 2001a)

The failure to make an explicit statement about the scale of adult provision runs counter to many of the pronouncements on lifelong learning in earlier documents and puts in doubt the cause of widening participation they appeared so eagerly to espouse.

The rationale for the concentration on the 16-19 cohort may be the assumption that a rise in staying-on rates among younger adults will lead to increased participation in later life. According to some analysts, this belief is unfounded. Gorard (2000a) for instance argues that prolonged initial education does not necessarily lead to later participation. He cites the findings of a large-scale household survey in South Wales which showed that although successive age cohorts are staying at school longer and obtaining higher levels of qualification, they tend not to continue to accumulate learning after the initial stage.

A similar conclusion was reached by Field (2001a) whose analysis of Labour Force Survey data suggested that participation in learning has risen among those aged 16+ but there has not been a corresponding rise among those aged over 25.

The lack of a strong focus on adults in educational policy will make a real change in participation patterns difficult to achieve.

Continuing primacy of instrumental and economic outcomes

There have been continuing debates over the last few decades about what constitutes 'useful' or 'relevant' learning, particularly in relation to what is eligible for public or employer support (Hillage *et al*, 2000).

Despite acknowledgment of the broader aims and value of education in policy, it is still viewed largely as a process to increase individual 'employability'. The breadth of vision in David Blunkett's much-admired and frequently quoted Foreword to the Green Paper *The Learning Age* (DfEE, 1998)[2] was contradicted by the subsequent narrowness of purpose summed up in the claim that lifelong learning is a way of 'putting jobs, skills and employability at the heart of Europe'. As many have observed, the overall emphasis in *The Learning Age*, as in the White Paper *Learning to Succeed* (DfEE, 1999a), was on education as a route to work:

> *When subjected to closer inspection, much of the policy interest in lifelong learning is in fact preoccupied with the development of a more productive and efficient workforce'.* (Field, 2000: viii)

---

2 'As well as securing our economic future, learning has a wider contribution. It helps make ours a civilised society, develops the spiritual side of our lives and promoted active citizenship. Learning enables people to play a full part in their community. It strengthens the family, the neighbourhood and consequently the nation. It helps us fulfil our potential and opens doors to a love of music, art and literature. That is why we value learning for its own sake as well as for the equality of opportunity it brings.' (Extract from *The Learning Age*, DfEE, 1998)

This focus informed the design of the new framework for post-16 education and training. The intention was to give employers the largest voice in the Learning and Skills Councils, and a 'key objective' for the new structure is 'to improve at both national and local level the quality of information about employer demand and employer needs that would go into the process of planning for provision'.[3] Forty per cent of representatives on the Local Learning and Skills Councils are from the business sector and many people formerly in Training and Enterprise Council (TEC) executive posts are also well represented.

There is a danger, therefore, that the widening participation agenda may be swallowed up in the skills agenda. One interviewee commented on the significance of the fact that there was no Policy Action Team set up for lifelong learning although one was set up for 'skills'.

Several assumptions underlie the continuing policy emphasis on employment and employability: that learning is undertaken primarily in order to achieve material rewards and a better standard of living and that learning automatically leads to jobs. Rees et al (1997) argue that the human capital theory upon which such assumptions are based is unsound as learning opportunities are not evenly distributed and people may have aims other than those related to material benefits. They point out that education and training 'opportunities' 'may well not be construed as such by potential trainees or employees' (p495).

This is borne out by research findings indicating that people's learning preferences, motivations and behaviour do not always coincide with the beliefs and assumptions of policy-makers:

> *In our study some people did not emphasise material rewards but instead focused on some other form of personal fulfilment, such as maximising personal interest and involvement through enjoyment, or as simply coping in order to survive. They associated these other types of motivation with their choice not to access some of the provision that was apparently open to them. Also other activities were seen as preferable, such as becoming focused on their role as parents or doing voluntary work. These were identified as alternative routes to the fulfilment interviewees were seeking.* (Bowman *et al*, 2000: 38-39)

The Bowman *et al* study highlighted the gap between many people's experiences and the 'simplistic' assumption that increased education and qualifications will automatically lead to employment and therefore improved life conditions. The researchers found that many interviewees did not see clear links between educational achievement and work opportunities. Their experience was that the range of work

---

3 Nick Stuart, Director General of Lifelong Learning, in conversation with Richard Ingham, *Individual Learning News*, Summer 2000 issue, pp2-3.

opportunities available to them was often restricted; that qualifications were not always valued and recognised; and that employers often discriminated arbitrarily against certain applicants and appointed people for reasons other than their qualifications:

> *The key characteristics of current social policy are: work is seen as the central means through which social policy will be pursued {and} individuals themselves are given the main responsibility for improving their conditions of life by taking advantage of training and employment opportunities voluntarily. The mechanisms through which policy operates are: responsibility for engaging in education and training to that end, even though the education system may have cast them as failures and the job market may reject or marginalise them.*

> *In our study interviewees believed that employers often recruited on some other basis than qualifications, namely experience or through personal networks, or using some idiosyncratic notion of personal qualities, and that they did not necessarily value certain qualifications at all.*

> *Some of the people interviewed during the research did not consider that education and training was the preferred route to employment. Others had found through their experiences of participating in government schemes that the opportunities actually open to them differed significantly from those claimed by policy makers, education providers and benefit advisors. (...) These findings led the researchers to conclude that current policy assumptions have little to do with many people's daily realities.* (pp38-39)

My own research into the outcomes of training programmes for unemployed groups in Coventry (McGivney and Thomson, 1995) produced similar findings. The major problem facing trainees after completion of courses was repeatedly identified as the lack of employment opportunities. Those who had obtained job interviews were often confused by the messages they had received. Sometimes they had been told they had too little experience; at other times that they were overqualified. Such experiences had led some to conclude that either employers did not know what they were looking for or that they were using over- or under-qualification as an excuse to discriminate against candidates on other grounds such as age, gender, parental status, race, length of unemployment or postcode. Many had experienced ageism and racism in job recruitment while women returners felt that the energy, motivation and organisational skills they had demonstrated in caring for families and undertaking training were not recognised by employers.

Other problems identified by trainees were the short term-nature of many jobs and the fact that the transition from unemployment benefit to a low-waged, short-term job often involved considerable financial and practical problems.

The Coventry study suggested that even if people do participate in education and training, it will not necessarily increase their 'employability' if they have characteristics considered undesirable by employers. There are still very real barriers such as employer prejudice, the paucity of jobs and the short-term and the low-paid nature of many of the jobs available.

> *On the one hand the literature preaches inclusiveness whilst on the other the real world practises exclusiveness.* (Cavanagh, 2000: 35)

Another assumption underlying policy discourses is that everyone has similar needs and opportunities. This ignores the huge regional and local differences in economic circumstances as well as in the availability of jobs and educational resources. As stressed by Bamber *et al* (2000), however, you cannot separate learning from the context in which it takes place. Local economic and social circumstances, for example, can engender sceptical views about the value of education and training (Ecclestone, 2001). Those who have experienced exclusion from the labour market are particularly sceptical about the alleged link between qualifications and jobs:

> *While there is no lack of desire by ethnic minorities to pursue further study, credentials do not improve the status of minorities as readily as whites, pointing to discrimination in the labour market.* (Robertson, 1997a: 9)

> *There are loads of people in our {Afro-Caribbean} community with pieces of paper but they still can't get a job.* (Informant)

Because of ageism in the labour market many mature students are also unconvinced that participation will produce a financial pay-off. (Callender, 1999)

The economic pay off from lower level qualifications is particularly questionable:

> *Advocacy of lifelong learning is based on the blanket assertion that all learning will pay off in terms of both personal fulfilment and wider economic outcomes. If this is true, it is hard to see why people are not banging on the doors of our learning institutions. (...) Research from the Centre for the Economics of Education will confirm that the rewards in terms of access to better paid jobs are generally high for those with good GCSE results and significantly better for those with A-levels and degrees. There are also healthy returns on vocational qualifications such as the HND and BTEC National. However, lower level qualifications, including NVQs at Levels 1 and 2 and the BTEC Firsts, appear to secure no increase in earnings. (...) Although lower attainment in literacy and numeracy is clearly associated with discrimination in the labour market, we have no evidence that obtaining basic skills qualifications attenuates that disadvantage.* (Robinson, 2000)

Continuing emphasis on linear progression

Despite these arguments, the policy emphasis on accreditation and nationally recognised qualifications remains as strong as ever. While *Learning to Succeed* (DfEE, 1999a) recognised the unsuitability of formal delivery for many people and the need for some non-accredited learning, it went on to state:

> *we would expect the {Learning and Skills Council} to give priority to courses that lead to nationally recognised qualifications and – more generally – to encourage learning towards recognised qualifications.* (p48)

Although the Schedule 2 divide has been removed and courses not leading to qualifications, or leading to qualifications which are not QCA-accredited, are eligible for funding: 'a strategic policy decision for the Learning and Skills Council was the proportion of funds that would be allocated to qualification-bearing targets in the context of national targets' (*FEFC Council News*, 2000).

In the Learning and Skills Act, two terms are used to describe recognised provision – 'qualifications', which refers to all the approved qualifications listed under Sections 96 and 97, and 'other' which refers to all other provision. Turner (2001) points out that since nearly 70 per cent of adult learners participate in programmes that do *not* lead to the approved qualifications, this means that the vast majority of programmes taken by adults are defined as 'other', including non-accredited courses and those leading to external awards and institutional certificates. The rather dismissive categorisation of such a wide range of learning programmes as 'other' reflects the lesser value attached to these in policy.

Despite the stress in earlier policy documents on community-based learning and the importance of meeting learner preferences, it is not yet clear whether non-accredited programmes will be formula-funded or dependent mainly on the discretionary funds – worth 10-15 per cent of overall LSC funds – available to the Local Learning and Skills Councils. These flexible budgets can be used for so many purposes besides adult and community learning and widening participation initiatives – marketing and promotion, workforce development (including Investors in People), Information and Guidance, small-scale local projects, regeneration initiatives, match funding for ESF and/or SRB – that informal, community-based projects could well be squeezed out. There is, however, a danger that innovative informal and non-accredited activities may be restricted to these budgets which, when shared between the 47 local councils, may not go very far.

Thus there are two key questions that have implications for wider participation – to what extent will less formal, non-accredited learning be supported by the LSC and to what extent will the local councils recognise achievements other than qualifications?[1] Section 3 of DfEE's Guidance to Learning Partnerships (DfEE, 2000c) recommends that adults should be offered a wide curriculum with a balance between recreational, academic and vocational learning, learning for personal and family growth (including basic and key skills) and learning to enhance the capacity of communities. But will such a balance be achieved given the powerful emphases on improving basic skills and meeting local employer needs? Unless a wide range of flexible and non-accredited opportunities is provided, however, there will be little chance of engaging significant numbers of people from the most disadvantaged groups in learning.

The official attachment to qualifications approved by the Qualifications and Curriculum Agency (QCA) could also be a serious block to wider participation. There is ambivalence in official circles about the flexible and learner-centred accreditation developed by the Open College Networks and doubts about the status and standards of Open College awards. As one informant put it, 'Do you only become a "real" student when you get the "real" qualifications?'. Robertson (1997b) has argued that the QCA standards framework may hinder rather than encourage wider participation:

> *The answer {to social imbalances in HE} is not to pursue the linguistic artificiality of 'standards frameworks' as if an assembly of language statements which purport to describe qualifications can materially influence institutional behaviour towards equitable participation. Nor can frameworks of any kind convincingly improve the welfare of individual learners unless they facilitate student transactions based explicitly on access, choice and mobility – in other words, on learners' preferences. Otherwise, they merely serve to police entry, progression and achievement in a higher education system increasingly disinclined to redefine itself flexibly or openly.* (pp24-25)

Some fear that the priority given to courses leading to nationally recognised qualifications: 'may result in a rush to accredit learning which should not be accredited and general adult education being treated as second class, to be paid for only after the "important" vocational courses' (NIACE, 1999: 8). This, of course, would be a re-run of what happened after 1992.

The emphasis on qualifications as evidence of achievement reflects the fact that policy continues to perceive learning mainly as an individual and vertical process. There is little recognition of shared and collective learning needs or the nature of adult participation. This is something that concerns many practitioners and analysts:

---

1 Since this was written the LSC has commissioned the Learning and Skills Development Agency to devise a national methodology for recording achievement in non-accredited learning.

New Labour's ideology is fundamentally individualist rather than collective (…) the result is to exclude consideration of the collective, the group needs (…) The policy and its implementation articulates this perspective clearly. HEFC's welcome initiatives in the late 1990s on widening participation are focused almost entirely upon the individual's accessibility and progression. (Taylor, 2000: 76-77)

The stress on qualifications and individual progression ignores the benefits of learning that are less easily measured such as more positive attitudes and spin-offs for communities and families. As I argued in my study of outreach (McGivney 2000a), criteria for effectiveness that only take into account student numbers, educational progression and employment outcomes fail to recognise that there are sometimes far more valuable gains for the wider community. Two further education colleges cited in that study found that participation did not always result in educational progression for individuals but often achieved very positive changes within their families:

When we did Nutrition for Travellers only one went into FE, but the kids' nutrition improved immeasurably.

A lot of local schools say that their OFSTED reports have been much better than expected. There are positive spin-offs from parents learning.

Tension between widening participation and the standards agenda

The current importance attached to learning outcomes and quality assurance is not easily reconcilable with the greater flexibility and learner-centredness required in order to widen participation in learning. Although the Learning and Skills Councils have been directed to pay attention to the wishes and needs of learners, they have many other priorities – to meet national learning targets for post-16, to raise the skills of the working population, to help to improve local labour markets and to raise the standards of provider performance. There is a strong danger that that the widening participation agenda may be overwhelmed by these other priorities.

The imposition of targets may also work against wider participation. Colleges have been required to set and monitor progress towards retention and achievement targets at both course and institutional level. An unintended consequence of this could be a reluctance to recruit students who seem unlikely to achieve.

Thus some of the measures to bring more people in learning may be neutralised by criteria to do with standards and achievements that may well have the effect of keeping them out. This tension is at its strongest in higher education where there is simultaneous pressure on institutions to increase student numbers and widen participation, to reduce non-completion rates; to become more accessible to under-represented groups; and also to become centres of research excellence. Some institutions find these demands irreconcilable:

> *As national policy is encouraging higher education to be more open and responsive to individual needs, institutional policy, under the pressure of rigorous quality assurance processes, is often unsympathetic to flexible educational practices.* (Rockhill, 1996: 192)

The tension between the widening participation agenda and other pressures on HEIs has been frequently noted. In many institutions the Research Assessment Exercise (RAE) and the drive to maintain standards take precedence over widening participation: 'the cult of the RAE drives academic behaviour more powerfully than student expansion' (*Times Higher*, 2001).

Woodrow (2000b) has commented on the fact that although HEFCE funding for widening participation has significantly increased, it is more than 25 times less than funding based on research. Inevitably, therefore, many universities are putting more effort into research production than into ensuring equality of access:

> *A major question must exist about the possibility of attracting, teaching, guiding and supporting a significant number of non-traditional students in a university so clearly focused on other, more powerful, and potentially overwhelming, priorities.* (Johnston and Croft, 1998)

Good RAE ratings also ensure that the older, more prestigious universities maintain their elite status whereas those which put most effort into broadening their intake risk having higher drop-out rates and falling to a lower position in the league tables.

> *By systematically weighting funding, the funding councils may encourage HEIs to make themselves more accessible to students from hitherto poorly represented groups. However, the real prizes and international prestige still lie with an institution's ability to attract research funding and maximise the 'R' element. While an elite of older universities will inevitably continue to corral most of these funds, most former polytechnics and colleges of HE will have to content themselves with increased widening participation funding, thus reopening the possibility of a new binary divide.* (Ward and Steele, 1999: 202-203)

Robertson (1997b) has detected a resistance in some (older) institutions and among some sections of society towards the whole concept of creating a more inclusive student body, as reflected in '*the apparently orchestrated assault by sections of the national press on the non-standard admissions policies of some universities during the summer of 1995*' (p24). And rumblings persist about wider access leading to 'dumbing-down', although lower achievement rates may relate more to the financial difficulties of poorer students than to lack of ability.

Over-reliance on ICT as a means of widening participation

A huge amount of political attention and central funding is being directed to the development of ICT strategies and ICT learning centres, the assumption being that these will increase and widen participation. Many find this assumption questionable, not least because of the wide disparities in access to computers: approximately 15 to 20 per cent of the population cannot use a computer and do not believe that ICT is relevant to them (Clarke, 2001). Moreover, although ICT-based learning may remove some of the barriers to participation, it cannot remove them all.

> *Not everyone has access. There's a very high drop-out rate and at least 20 per cent of the population (many of them among the hardest to reach) are resistant to it. They see it negatively as leading to loss of jobs or as associated with drop in skills (like calculators). The digital divide also exists among the more affluent parts of society who choose to ignore IT.* (Informant)

> *The culture of ICT (…) is young, white, middle-class and male; precisely the narrow attributes of the traditional adult learning base the government is so keen to move beyond. Many of the technologies used to deliver learning (the Internet, etc) are not necessarily dominant or familiar technology with the working-class, older, female, ethnic learner. Access to computers, both at home and at work, is significantly more common among men, occupational classes A and B, those who left full-time continuous education later, and those with higher qualifications. Access is less likely for those aged 55 or more, retired, unemployed and those otherwise not working.* (Gorard, 2000b: 189)

Although UfI, the establishment of learndirect centres and other measures involving ICT are improving the overall *spread* of learning resources, many people such as those in some rural areas and, particularly, the elderly are still largely neglected.

There is also concern that that the increasing shift to resource-based learning may result in insufficient human support for widening participation:

> *The 'customer care' side of learning centres will be crucial.* (Interviewee)

> *Too much policy sees ICT as a substitute for teaching, not as a supplement to it. But the kind of widening participation students we're talking about – you can't just bang them off to an ICT centre. A lot will be left to flounder. They'll just be turned off again.* (Interviewee)

Lack of attention to human as well as on-line support could explain the low completion and achievement rates in ICT learning. According to FEFC (2000a) it is not uncommon to find achievement rates of under 20 per cent among those taking open and distance learning programmes using IT-based materials in colleges.

Fox (2001) argues that those who are promoting ICT as revolutionising the learning process often conflate the tool with the end product. Moreover, although ICT learning materials should be tailored to the needs of specific groups of learners, it is feared that programmes will tend to be uniform regardless of learners' gender, ethnicity, socio-economic status, age and physical location. ICT and opportunities for open learning also reinforce the stress on individual learning processes and progression:

> *Learning is presented as an essentially individualised process (…). There is no sense of the necessity to explore ideas with others, to engage in challenging discussions, to explore alternative interpretations of the information provided in 'the package'. Nor is there any sense of the opportunity to share and discuss ideas with, or observe other students. (…) It seems paradoxical that the rationale (…) is so clearly linked to access and participation, yet the very education that is being accessed may be quite emaciated and devoid of cultural diversity.* (Morrison, 1995: 128)

A number of analysts therefore feel that the faith in ICT is unfounded and that it will not encourage the most excluded groups to engage in structured learning in the way anticipated by Government. Citing evidence from a number of surveys, Field (2000) concludes that a dramatic shift towards the use of new technologies to promote self-directed learning appears unlikely:

> *What is clear at this stage is that the most reluctant learners, and the most excluded and peripheral groups within the workforce more generally, are unlikely to embrace learning through ICT any more than they are attracted by more conventional approaches.* (p99)

Moreover, case studies from 86 colleges have shown that face-to-face contact and personal tutoring are far more effective in improving achievement and retention than IT, distance learning and self study (Martinez, 2001).

Anomalies in student support

Despite the plethora of widening participation initiatives in higher education, there is evidence that the withdrawal of the maintenance grant and its replacement by loans, together with the imposition of tuition fees, have deterred many mature learners and lower income groups from applying to higher education. According to UCAS (Universities and Colleges Admissions Service) 1998 admissions data, there was a 10,000 decrease in the number of students over the age of 21 entering HE compared with the previous year. Ward and Steele (1999) point out that at the very time when the Government and funding councils were developing policies and programmes to widen participation, the social imbalance in participation was intensifying rather than lessening. In 1998 only 2.2 per cent of applicants were from unskilled backgrounds, whereas 43.7 per cent were from managerial or technical backgrounds. The proportion of all applicants from the top two social classes actually increased between 1997 and 1998:

> *The government followed its predecessor's policy of phasing out maintenance grants and offering loans in their place. But don't bother to apply if you are over 50. Nor did the government restore the mature students allowance phased out two years earlier. On top of this it followed the lead of many other countries in imposing tuition fees but with exemption for households earning less than £16k and on a scale up to £23k. Not surprisingly, many working-class adults initially attracted by the rhetoric of widening participation who were contemplating entering university through access courses and other routes are thinking again and UCAS applications from adults are down by around 12%.* (Steele, 1999: 22-23)

Applications from people over 21 have recently started to rise again. Goddard (2001) quotes an UCAS report saying that mature student applications were up by 4.7% last year following the introduction of a £1,000 grant for travel and childcare (replaced in September 2001 by a grant covering up to 85 per cent of the costs of childcare). However, the same article includes a quote from the president of the National Union of Students citing figures from the Higher Education Statistics Agency showing that actual enrolments for this group had dropped by 26 per cent since 1997.

Thus, as suggested by Callender and Kemp (2001) in their report on student finances, government policies seem to be at odds with their own widening participation agenda, since the very people whom they wish to attract are those most deterred by costs and fear of debt. This has had a knock-on effect on some institutions, especially in London where universities with a large proportion of mature students have been hard hit by the lower number of applications.

Woodrow (2000b) argues that some of the recent changes in student support such as hardship loans and Access funds represent a process closer to 19th than to 21st Century social policy – a view that is shared by other commentators:

> *Hardship loans and access funds, awarded in a piecemeal manner to the poorest students, cap-in-hand, form a system more akin to Dickensian philanthropy than an efficient means of targeting need without humiliation and financial insecurity.* (Boyson, 2000)

Proposals for applying differential fees for different courses that are periodically put forward by some universities have aroused fears that such a move would accentuate social divisions in the sector and force poorer students to apply for the cheapest courses (Boyson, 2000).

Partnerships

Although the huge increase in collaboration and partnerships that has occurred over the last five years is welcome, partnerships on their own will not bring about wider participation especially if the principal aim is to access central funding. According to one informant, some institutions: 'want the funding but they don't really want to work with anyone else'. Others have found that as much if not more is spent on the actual servicing and running of partnerships as on strategies to widen participation.

There is also a question about whether the shift to partnerships will be strong enough to overcome the culture of competition that developed in both the further and the higher education sectors during the 1990s.

Neglect of the voluntary sector

Some of the new partnerships are unequal. They are usually dominated by the larger education institutions and the voluntary sector is often ignored, taken advantage of or left out of the decision-making process altogether:

Smaller organisations are suspicious of larger ones. You're expecting the sheep to lie down with the lions but they'll just get eaten. (Informant)

The voluntary sector don't think things have got any better. (Interviewee)

There is a contradiction between the stress on community-inspired and -managed learning in policy documents and the actual marginalisation of the voluntary sector in policy measures. Despite references to the importance of the contribution of voluntary and community organisations to 'first-rung' provision and the regeneration of communities: 'there has been little evidence of any concrete new approaches to engaging the sector in the structures being created' (Lochrie, 2001: 11). 'The representation of the sector in LSC appointments has been virtually minimal' (Turner, 2000).

There are also fears that LSC requirements will put some community-based and voluntary sector providers out of business. Under the new structure, new learning providers have to comply with a set of national quality criteria which some will be unable to meet:

There's a direct issue about widening participation versus concentration on achievement and credentialism. This will affect the voluntary sector under LSC very heavily. They will have to do all the things that traditional providers do (demonstrate achievement, etc) and they're very worried about that. (Interviewee)

According to several reports (Hook, 2001; *Working Brief*, 2001b(c)), the reduction in the budget for work-based learning for adults has meant that some of the smaller, community-rooted organisations experienced in assisting people with multiple barriers to learning have not been awarded tenders and resources are being concentrated on larger providers. *Working Brief* also reports that the LSC requires providers to operate within very tight margins of income, restricting on-programme payments to set lengths of stay that are unrealistic for learners who take longer to achieve:

> *Faced by a rigid funding formula which pays out the same programme rates regardless of the circumstances in which training is delivered, providers warn that they may be forced to scale back the volume of provision they deliver or at least reduce the support in the form of outreach work and pastoral care they can offer learners.* (p17)

Boyer (2001) also warns that we risk losing good community-based providers with experience in supporting the most excluded groups, and this has implications for the capacity of the LSC to meet the targets it has been set by Government. A system that is weighted too much in favour of larger providers will not be conducive to wider participation in learning. To engage new groups will require an expansion rather than a contraction of the number of routes through which people can access learning. It will require a strong and diverse provider base (Boyer, 2001) and provision of a range of small-scale opportunities of the kind often provided by community and voluntary organisations.

* * *

As in the early 1990s, therefore, policy measures have been having both a push and a pull effect on adult participation with advances in some areas being restricted or cancelled out by other policies or different aspects of the same measures. Consequently there is a danger that, in terms of changing the profile of adult learners, we may end up where we started. Even the measures with most apparent potential for widening participation may not achieve their objectives. To take just five examples:

Postcodes

Although use of postcode targeting is a very positive move, such a measure cannot identify the pockets of disadvantage within more prosperous areas. This means that applications for funding from some areas of deprivation are routinely turned down because of their location.

The postcode model is useful but it's too blunt an instrument to pick this up. The difficulty for the government and providers is that funding is finite, therefore you need to set priorities. It is understandable that funding needs to go to hard 'nodules' of disadvantage for maximum effect. But the problems with targeting are: it's always crude and there are groups on the margins of problems areas who miss out because they're not quite disadvantaged enough. And all targeting misses the point about core facilities. (Interviewee).

ILAs

These, according to one interviewee, 'have had the absolutely foreseeable effect of putting up the price of courses, as providers match prices to what an ILA might buy'[3]

There are also some worries about the restrictions placed on the kind of learning activities the accounts can be used for: 'is this the re-emergence of the vocational/non vocational divide? I see problems on the horizon'. (Interviewee)

Moves to widen participation in HE

As has so often happened in the past, some of the new measures in place to encourage a wider mix of people to enter university are still tending to attract individuals from more affluent, middle-class backgrounds. Baty (2000) reports that more privileged children have been filling places on the Government's Excellence in Cities initiative because schools have been asked to target their top 10 per cent achievers and too few students from deprived backgrounds meet the criteria:

Middle-class young people with a family tradition of university education have been taking places on summer schools designed to widen access to lower income and deprived groups. Schools are putting forward their high-fliers and best candidates.

Reservations have also been expressed about the use of adjusted sector benchmarks to judge the success of individual institutions in widening participation. Woodrow,[4] for example, feels that this will reinforce and legitimise the *status quo* in respect of variations in institutional student profiles. She questions whether benchmarks should be based on subject areas as this could suggest that is acceptable for some subjects to exclude some groups and could lead to some professions maintaining their elitism. There is also concern about the setting of differential widening

---

3 ILAs were suspended in October 2001 following allegations of fraud.
4 Maggie Woodrow, presentation at meeting of SRHE Access groups on access performance indicators, October 1999.

participation rates for institutions as this could widen the gap between them and allow the sector to become increasingly polarised along social class lines.

Stress on literacy, numeracy and ESOL skills

Although the national strategy to improve literacy, numeracy and English language (ESOL) skills has been widely welcomed, it is not necessarily the most effective tool for widening participation as not everybody who does not engage in organised learning has poor basic or English language skills. Moreover, this focus tends to highlight people's learning deficits and implies a limited view of provision for non-participating adults as remedial or compensatory. This will not necessarily be the best way of engaging people in learning, especially if there is an element of coercion:

If they haven't done well at school giving them more of the same in the adult sector isn't going to work. (Interviewee)

The notion of compulsory testing in order to tell people how badly they're doing is ridiculous. (Interviewee)

Interviewees made a clear distinction between the enforcement of education and the choice to learn, associating enforcement with school and many Benefit-related options. (Bowman *et al*, 2000: 39)

Adult and Community Learning Fund

The Adult and Community Learning Fund (ACLF) has been one of the most effective measures for developing innovative, community-based learning activities with the groups least likely to enter formal education. However, the limited funding available has meant that only a few hundred projects have received funding over the four years that the fund has been in existence. It has been announced that the fund will be extended, but in order to make a real difference to overall adult participation patterns it will need to be substantially greater than it has been.

Similarly the Community Development Learning Fund, though very useful, involves very small sums (£250-£3,000) and requires local impact in a short period.

* * *

Some of the contradictions in policy can be attributed to the haste in which successive measures have been introduced. Indeed, it has been hard at times to keep up with the tidal wave of measures and initiatives that have been introduced in post-16 education since 1997:

Typically what service planners are doing is trying to meet too many priorities and too many target groups. So many attempts to engage people are hit and miss. (Interviewee)

If they're so keen on standards, the Government's own policy initiatives need to be held up to scrutiny. Everything they're doing is in too much haste, for example Ufl and the lack of consultation with FE; lack of appropriate time scales and inappropriate course materials. (Interviewee)

Many now feel that there is a need for a halt or interval in order to consolidate and reflect on developments to date:

What we may be learning is that institutional reform, endless initiatives and rhetoric about lifelong learning do not guarantee improved outcomes. (Robinson, 2000)

There is universal appreciation of change of climate, one in which you can speak of widening participation and it is a legitimate concern and goal. But there is also a strong view that too much is being 'loaded' onto lifelong learning and widening participation and that the people driving these agendas are in too much of a hurry so they could backfire if they don't achieve rapid and visible results. (Gorard, 2000a: 6)

The weariness of some practitioners was illustrated at a NIACE conference in 2000 at which a minister – whose address had been lavishly sprinkled with words such as 'innovative', 'imaginative' and 'creative' in relation to learning opportunities – was taken to task by a delegate who retorted: 'We're sick of having to innovate and do something new. Can't we build on the successes we already have?' (Let us also note that providers are constantly called upon to innovate whereas policy-makers them-selves are very conservative and wary of innovation.)

Overall, therefore, current measures seem unlikely to bring about the step changes in participation that have been called for in policy documents and I would single out five major reasons why the profile of adult learners is unlikely to be significantly changed in the foreseeable future:

First, many laudable moves to widen participation are being cancelled out by attempts to raise standards and achievement levels which go far beyond even those of the previous Government.

Second, there is the conspicuous absence in centrally-directed widening participa-tion measures of policies to assist the participation of older adults (or even not so old ones, as it is still difficult for learners over 50 to obtain financial support). This suggests that people who have left the labour market or who are at the end of their working lives are not considered important, which not only goes against all principles of social justice, but is also extremely short-sighted, given the increasing numbers of older adults in the population.

Third, the continuing reluctance to put pressure on employers to provide training opportunities or study leave: 'the failure to make employers shape up; to ensure an obligatory framework ensuring opportunities at work is the worst of failures' (Interviewee).

Fourth, the continuing lack of recognition of, and support for, collective informal learning:

> *David Blunkett in his Foreword to the White Paper argues that 'we must place the learner at the heart of the new system' (DfEE, 1999a). The learner in question would appear to be an employable adult of working age on a formal course leading to a recognised qualification. The case for informal learning has not only still to be won, it has scarcely begun to be heard.* (Coffield 2000b: 10)

Fifth, innovative, informal community-based work of a kind most likely to attract new learners is still accorded lower priority than accredited and formal learning, and continues to be reliant on special measures and short-term initiative funding which is always oversubscribed (Bell, 1999). Thus, while on the one hand locally-based and locally-inspired work is being strongly encouraged, on the other it continues to be undervalued and under-supported. This ensures that little of a long-term nature can be achieved and that widening participation initiatives stay outside or on the periphery of mainstream education. The evaluation of Non-Schedule 2 pilots found little evidence that the projects were having any impact upon institutional curriculum planning and delivery (Greenwood *et al*, 2000). In this respect little appears to have changed since the late 1980s when I found that the majority of initiatives and learning activities directed at the groups least represented in mainstream provision were specially-funded programmes, a fact which simultaneously labelled them as priority areas and as areas peripheral to 'normal' or mainstream provision (McGivney, 1990).

What seems have happened since 1998 is that the stress on widening participation has quietly slipped down the list of priorities and been subsumed within related concerns (such as poor basic skills in the adult population). In a conference presentation in May 2001, John Harwood, Chief Executive of the LSC, itemised the main goals of the new structure as: to encourage more young people to achieve Level 2; to maximise the contribution of education and training to economic performance; to raise standards, and to increase demand for learning – in that order.[5] Moreover, it is not yet clear to what extent widening participation will figure in the common inspection framework.

In consequence, it may not be in post-16 education but through measures to bring about neighbourhood renewal that any significant changes in adult participa-

---

5 Presentation to NIACE conference 'Increasing Demand for Learning', London, 10 May 2001.

tion will be achieved. Some feel that the most interesting initiative instigated by the current Government has been the Social Exclusion Unit. The work of 18 cross-departmental policy and action teams (PATs) and overall strategy, as set out in policy documents on neighbourhood renewal, have been examples of cross-departmental collaboration that have not been seen before. The reports produced for the unit, such as those from the Policy Action Teams, have gone further than any educational documents in recognising the need for a comprehensive approach to exclusion. Learning and development are at the heart of the Neighbourhood Renewal National Strategy Action Plan which proposes to encourage a learning habit among all the key players in neighbourhood renewal:

> *I feel more optimistic about the Neighbourhood Renewal strategy. That offers much more scope for flexibility than just getting basic skills right (although the educational indicator even there is about children getting GCSEs: nothing about adults).* (Interviewee)

If current measures to increase demand for learning are too timid or too overwhelmed by other priorities to bring about any real changes in the social profile of adult learners, what steps could be taken to widen participation in the post-16 system? The kind of changes that are needed in order to significantly change the overall profile of adult learners will be explored in the following chapter.

Chapter 8

Revising assumptions and strategies

What national and institutional strategies might attract adults from under-represented groups into organised learning?

National policy

Drawing on the lessons of the past

First, there is a need to build on what has happened before. There was good practice before 1997, and education and related policies should take account of the lessons from the stream of effective initiatives, programmes and projects stretching back over 30 years – developments in ILEA, the access movement, the REPLAN Programme, WEA programmes, residential college outreach and bespoke courses, and countless short-term projects in local education authorities, further education colleges and universities which have been described in course and research reports. Many of these have produced consistent findings about adult learning that continue to be ignored in policy, notably that:

- adults have very diverse reasons for returning to learning of which gaining employment and associated material rewards is only one;
- adult learning trajectories are not always linear and are often interrupted;
- learning is a social activity that is embedded in the family, social and community contexts in which people lead their lives;
- learning is often a shared rather than individual activity, conducted 'in cultural collectivities' (Davies, 2001: 3); and
- individuals cannot be abstracted from the class structures and cultural perspectives into which they have been conditioned and socialised.

Greater appreciation of these points would be an appropriate starting point for a serious re-consideration of the whole widening participation enterprise. In particular, there is a need to recognise the zigzag and discontinuous character of adult learning patterns:

> *Once people get through the doors of education provision they seem to be prepared to participate throughout their lives. One of the most striking things about the interviews was the sheer amount of time people had spent doing education or training of some sort or another, and the number of different courses and qualifications they had pursued throughout their lives (...). This does not mean though that once people have started to access education facilities they follow one path towards a long-term goal. Interviewees described how they had done several different and often unrelated courses leading up to the point at which they were interviewed. They suggested that there were various reasons for choosing to do courses at different times in their lives; this often meant that their education history was varied and patchy.* (Bowman et al, 2000: 23)

Addressing the contradictions

Next, there is a need to address some of the contradictions in current policy that are currently stymieing otherwise laudable attempts to widen participation.

Economic aims and social inclusion aims are not necessarily compatible and encouraging individuals to improve their skills and credentials will not necessarily bring about inclusion, given the paucity and low level of the jobs available in many deprived areas. Those most excluded from mainstream learning opportunities are often the same people who are excluded from reasonable employment opportunities. Logically, therefore, the policy stress on learning to improve individual employment prospects and meet employer needs should be accompanied by an equal focus on labour market initiatives:

> *Education and training policies need to be matched by labour market policies to ensure that those who participate in learning are rewarded in some way by the labour market for their efforts. Building a learning society requires more than supply-side policies. Piecemeal incentives to stimulate participation in lifelong learning and to make learning more accessible are unlikely on their own to bring about the real cultural change in attitudes to learning that the vision of a learning age demands. In order to bring about this kind of radical change, the Government will have to consider how it can ensure that the labour market both rewards the fruits of learning and encourages those who have gained higher skills to participate more fully in building the high skills economy which the Government claims it wishes to create.* (Hodgson and Spours, 1999: 20)

Another contradiction is the tension between the widening participation and standards agendas which will have to be resolved if attempts to achieve a more equitable system are not to be submerged in a rising tide of regulation and targets.

Standards need to fit around learners not just around audit culture:

> *I think every aspect of LSC system is going to reflect the tension between widening participation and raising standards. But there shouldn't be a contradiction. It's about definitions of quality. Will Ofsted really understand widening participation and which agenda will win out?* (Interviewee)

This is not to suggest that there should not be attention to quality. Criteria related to widening participation should be key aspects of quality assurance in all initiatives driven by central funding:

> *If you put enough money into widening participation they'll all do it. Whether it will be good quality is a different matter. If you reward it, colleges will do it. Look at franchising!* (Interviewee)

> *The good institutions will always do widening participation. The key is to put a floor to ensure that other institutions do it – the comfortable colleges serving comfortable areas with only pockets of disadvantage. They need to make some advance.* (Interviewee)

Quality criteria should not be restricted to accreditation and narrow interpretations of what constitutes 'progression' but should be designed to ensure that long-term and sustainable change actually takes place in the communities least represented in organised education. This means that *longer* timescales should be allowed for widening participation strategies:

> *It is our experience that almost any activity, in the short-term, can provide glowing evaluations from participants (often on the basis that whatever is done, it's far better than the nothing that existed previously); can shift attainment levels without worrying too much about whether these would have shifted anyway; can produce dazzling reports on work done with small numbers under relatively artificial conditions.*

> *It is much harder in the long haul:*

> - *to ensure that the thing done was the best possible use of time, energy and resources, out of the several things that could have been done.*
> - *to ensure that progress made is bigger, faster, deeper, wider, better etc, than would have happened anyway (...)*
> - *to ensure that real change is brought about for large numbers, in lasting ways, within the everyday ways of living, working and being.*
> (*Core Skill News*, 2000: 6).

A final contradiction that needs to be resolved is that between the policy stress on locally-based and -managed learning and the apparent lack of a real commitment to voluntary providers. To widen participation in many communities will require the cooperation of a range of community agencies and voluntary sector providers. Their involvement should be resourced and supported beyond token representation in local partnerships.

Revision of policy assumptions

There is also a need to revise some of the assumptions and preconceptions on which official views of widening participation are based. The fact that people do not engage in organised learning does not mean that they are non-learners. A wealth of socially and economically valuable learning is conducted outside organised provision.

Second, the groups least represented in organised learning do not all have remedial learning needs and the national campaign to improve adult basic skills should not overwhelm the entire widening participation agenda.

Third, there needs to be a re-examination of the preconceptions and stereotypes around notions of 'disadvantage' in financial measures to widen participation as they can lead to a competition to prove which groups are most deprived. Many of the people who do not engage in organised learning do not regard themselves as 'deprived', and some groups who would not be considered eligible for support may have less access to educational resources and opportunities than those identified as disadvantaged.

Fourth, 'lifelong' learning should mean just that and not apply only to people of working age. There should be strategies to include older adults, the shameful neglect of whom in recent policy has had a *'disastrous impact on third-age patterns of participation'* (Gorard, 2000a: 4).

Fifth, strategies involving ICT will not miraculously widen participation among those least represented in formal provision. Current ICT initiatives will only be as good as the materials used, the human as well as on-line support available and the opportunities offered for interactive learning. Their effectiveness will depend on ensuring synergy between technology and human interaction.

Sixth, qualifications, especially lower ones, do not automatically produce an economic pay-off and there are many other valuable and valued outcomes of learning. Wider participation is more likely to be achieved if the Learning and Skills Councils acknowledge the broader aims and benefits of learning, and do not impose inappropriate requirements for 'progression' on the learning they support. This implies the need to rethink what is meant by 'achievement' and 'progression'. Progression cannot be defined as a single direction or set of outcomes. It means different things to different people, depending on their characteristics, circum-stances and starting points. The increased confidence and recognition of potential gained during informal learning are often the benefits most highly prized by learners.

An important pre-requisite for changing adult participation patterns, therefore, would be to re-examine the ideas and assumptions on which current policies have been based.

Following that, there is a number of practical measures and changes that could bring about a change in the composition of adult participation.

Greater political focus on adult learning

From the point of view of national policy, a nationwide culture of learning will only be achieved when there is as strong a political focus on adults as there is on the 16-18 cohort. This means that greater priority should be given to the distribution, status and funding of learning opportunities for adults. This is an obvious point if statements about the desirability of 'lifelong' learning and building a learning society are to be meaningful.

If there is a genuine wish to widen participation in learning, then another basic requirement would be to tackle the uneven and inequitable distribution of adult learning opportunities. The Local Learning and Skills Councils should hopefully be able to eliminate some of the disparities between the learning resources available in different localities. However, strategies are also needed to address the variations in availability of workplace opportunities. We are frequently told that we lag behind other countries in skill levels but little is made of the fact that we also lag behind other countries in the extent to which workers are given opportunities to learn.

> *It is not only learners for whom the concept of lifelong learning has to be attractive; it also needs to be recognised, valued and supported by public and private employers, who have a key part to play in the practical realisation of the concept.* (Hodgson and Spours, 1999: 19)

> *The failure to train is the biggest challenge in creating a learning society. It is one which employers and government, rather than the education and training system, need to address urgently.* (Coffield, 2000c)

Various suggestions have been made on how to tackle this problem. There could be a minimal regulatory framework, as proposed by NAGCELL (1999), requiring all employers above a certain threshold to abide by a code of good practice for workplace learning, or there could be a significant extension of the entitlement to paid educational leave currently only available to workers aged 16-18 without 5 GCSEs, as proposed by the TUC and individual analyses (Mackney, 2000). Other measures that have frequently been suggested are tax incentives or penalties, or training levies to persuade employers to invest in training for all their workers including older workers, manual workers, part-time and temporary workers. Special measures are also needed to offer opportunities to workers in small and medium enterprises (SMEs) (as has already been recognised by Government[1]).

More generous resourcing of community learning

Some of the practical measures needed to produce a more equitable spread of local opportunities have been outlined by Price (2001) who calls for 'serious long-term money' for adult and community learning:

> *and I don't just mean a few computer terminals in supermarkets and advertising campaigns. It we are intent upon widening participation we need to establish some well-resourced, locally accountable and focused facilities in the poorest neighbourhoods. We need facilities that engage with people, work in partnership and connect learning with overcoming social problems, meeting community aspirations and expressing frustrations. This isn't just about large, existing education providers doing a bit more 'outreach' with the so-called 'socially excluded' (...) It is about giving the most disadvantaged communities the educational tools to do the job on their terms. It implies a sustained commitment to ensuring less judgmental policy-making, less short-term, output-driven funding and a real end to the idiotic characterisation of some adult learning as meaningful and some as frivolous.* (p12)

To widen participation genuinely, the LSC will therefore need to ensure that the same level of support is provided for informal and non-accredited programmes as for other programmes; that the diversity of adult provision is maintained, and that a wide range of opportunities is available to adults.

We need a funding system that that treats part-time and full-time learners equally; that gives parity to different learning goals and outcomes; that is adequate to cover the costs of development work with, and support for, learners; and that is sufficiently long-term to embed new practices and allow for the time it takes for learning habits to develop.

> *'You've got to have the patience to invest in people and let them put a toe in the water'.*
> (Interviewee)

Providers also need to be adequately compensated for the additional costs involved in attracting non-traditional participants and supporting them.

These lessons do not yet appear to have been fully learned. The evaluation of non-Schedule 2 pilots (Greenwood *et al*, 2000) found that the 5 per cent additional development costs offered by FEFC in addition to the unit-linked funding was considered insufficient, and although the funding level of programmes (Cost

---

1 See press release 446/00 17 Oct 2000, 'Blunkett offers extra financial help to small businesses'.

Weighting Factor C) was much appreciated, many found even this level of funding insufficient to support essential elements of projects such as outreach work and childcare.

The funding of provision for new groups of learners should not be dependent on the numbers of learners recruited, learning 'achievements' or educational progression. The evaluation of Non-Schedule 2 pilots concluded that a funding system based on the learners recruited will result in provider reluctance to invest time and resources in essential development work which cannot guarantee the desired outcomes (Greenwood *et al*, 2000). Moreover, providers may be deterred from targeting some groups if there is a danger of being financially penalised for low levels of achievement or non-completion. For some disadvantaged groups and localities, it is unrealistic to expect immediate outcomes in the form of movement to progressively more advanced levels of learning. It can take a long time to raise the confidence and aspirations of people in the most disadvantaged geographical areas and the results of learning may be slow to appear and may not be those that are expected:

> *The outcomes of non-accredited learning often manifest themselves in different ways to those anticipated and in different locations to the original learning situation. {LSC need to} take account of the delayed recognition of learning, the deferred moment of epiphany, the eventual use of a skill that takes place some time after the programme itself has finished.* (Turner, 2001: 8)

Support for widening participation initiatives should therefore be flexible enough to enable experiment and risk-taking: 'Less control doesn't necessarily mean chaos'[2].

The Local Councils could also allocate some separate and protected funding for community-based learning in further education as there may be principals who do not recognise the need for this work. They will also need to ensure that the funding for widening participation actually goes into work with local learners rather than into supporting partnership infrastructures. This means resourcing voluntary sector providers as well as large public sector providers.

Financial support for learners

Significant changes in adult participation patterns are more likely to be achieved through a coherent, flexible and equitable system of financial support for both full- and part-time learners, coordinated with the tax and benefit system, than through piecemeal initiatives that sometimes come into collision with benefit regulations:

---

2 Annette Zera, Principal of Tower Hamlets College, speaking at the NIACE National Conference on lifelong learning and neighbourhood renewal on 6 December 2000.

> *It is important to get tax and other financial incentives for individuals and employers right to encourage participation in education and training while, at the same time, ensuring that the benefit system works in tandem with education and training policy to support investment in learning.* (Hodgson and Spours, 1999: 21)

Some form of minimum entitlement up to Level 3 for all adults, especially those who are socially and economically deprived (a notion proposed in Kennedy, 1997), would also help to widen the learner profile. Some have also suggested the introduction of a learning allowance for adults out of the labour market who are undertaking learning to help their job prospects.

Fees for publicly-funded provision should be consistent across the country and providers should be resourced sufficiently to enable them to offer concessions:

> *LEAs are not sure whether they will be able to sustain concessions under the new funding systems. Fee income is a significant part of the service budgets of many LEAs. Fee income is reduced as provision becomes more targeted on the socially disadvantaged.* (Merton, 2001)

In addition to fee remission, learners in receipt of benefits and on the lowest incomes should be eligible for help with other costs such as those involved in transport, childcare, materials and examination fees.

The thorny issue of finance for higher education students needs also to be revisited as current measures are clearly acting as a deterrent to the social groups most unrepresented in the sector.[3]

Support for outreach activities

All the evidence shows that people who have not participated in structured learning programmes often do so as a result of face-to-face interventions from people whom they know and trust and who have local credibility. The Local Learning and Skills Councils are responsible for the Information and Guidance (IAG) partnerships and it is hoped they will encourage and support more community-based face-to-face provision of independent information, advice and guidance. However, if they also put resources into quality outreach work, that would be one of the most effective methods of widening participation among the most excluded groups. This would require investing in people with the necessary skills in networking with local communities. Such work should not be largely or totally reliant on short-term funding:

> *Those engaged professionally to support community development and capacity-building*

---

3 Since this was written the Government has announced a 'rethink' of higher education student support

should not so often be engaged on short-term contracts, be at the margins of the mainstream or be resourced only or largely through transient funding. Such an approach will neither embed the benefits nor represent an effective use of money. (NAGCELL, 1999)

If each of the Local Learning and Skills Councils were to appoint a team of local outreach workers, to work across all providers in the localities they cover, this might make a significant contribution towards achieving the locally-inspired provision called for in numerous policy statements.

Supporting informal learning

Ways should also be sought of supporting learning that takes place outside of prescribed frameworks and dedicated learning environments. Given that learning trajectories often originate in involvement in local issues, wider participation in organised learning can be achieved by making connections with local people and identifying their concerns: 'the trick in a national programme is to find a framework for linking with local concerns without losing the local aspect'. (Interviewee)

Recognising a range of learning achievements

There has been formal acknowledgement, not least in David Blunkett's Letter of Remit to the LSC, that, although qualifications are important, adults should be able to gain recognition for provision leading to other outcomes. This has been accepted by a number of post-16 agencies:

> *The Council wishes to see institutions formerly funded by the FEFC making full use of the opportunities offered by the legislation {repeal of S2} to introduce high quality, creative and innovative non-qualification bearing provision to reach out to new learners.* (FEFC, 2001: 5)

> *We want to see the LSC provide opportunities with scope for learners to gain recognition for their achievements other than through qualifications* (Adult Learning Inspectorate *et al*, 2001: 5.27).

Yet, as observed in Chapter 7, there are signs that it will be longer, qualification-bearing courses that will be given priority rather than shorter, non-accredited ones that are more likely to appeal to groups of new learners. Learning that improves one's chances in the labour market is obviously important, but so is learning that enriches us personally and culturally and which assists us in other dimensions of our lives – as parents, as citizens, as members of local communities and interest groups:

A genuine culture of lifelong learning needs to adopt a very broad definition of learning which includes general education, education for living and for active citizenship; improving the skills of the workforce must not become the only or the overriding goal of policy. Many adults, and especially those who have retired, wish to take a broad range of courses and they neither need nor want a qualification. Insisting that such courses become accredited may alienate these learners. (Coffield, 2000b: 7)

A learning society isn't just an accredited society. We need a broad and generous definition of lifelong learning in order to widen participation. We need learning that is formal or informal, at home or at work, in your neighbourhood or via your TV, certificated or not and that, most importantly, always connects directly with your life and your concerns (...). A learning society that is a Gradgrind training camp for a flexible labour force (...) is essentially a contradiction in terms. (Price, 2001: 12)

We should not, however, polarise the accreditation debate. Accreditation recognises individual achievement and we have to accept that many individuals who get involved in community learning eventually want to engage in learning that is formally recognised. Optional accreditation, as currently offered in many informal learning programmes (and in UfI programmes) is a good compromise, so long as it is not given precedence over the learning that is non-accredited:

We need a more sophisticated debate about accreditation that doesn't fall into the two opposing camps – 'it values learner achievements and gives self-esteem' versus 'it alienates and demotivates'. Are we about to have another re-run of this with LSC? Kennedy ducked the issue but substituted it by saying non-formal learning is fine as long as it leads to formal. (Interviewee).

At the same time we need to find new ways of measuring learning achievement, perhaps by borrowing some of the measures used in other sectors, and by looking at the impact of adult learning not only on the economy, but also on social, mental and physical health, the environment, civil society, and so on. One of the problems, however, is finding a means of encapsulating and reporting the qualitative outcomes in a way that will persuade policy-makers of their value. Promisingly, several initiatives commissioned by the former DfEE and LSC are underway to identify and describe learning achievements, outcomes and benefits.

Integrating education policies with those designed to eradicate poverty and disadvantage

To widen participation in learning we need to recognise just how deep the economic, social and cultural divides in society actually are. What has become increasingly clear is that you cannot divorce learning from the overall context of people's lives.

Under-representation in organised learning is just one dimension of the multiple and inter-related forms of social exclusion that many people face. Thus to achieve the 'step-change' in participation called for in so many policy documents, there needs to be some articulation between initiatives to widen participation and those designed to combat poverty and exclusion. In other words, educational planning and learning opportunities need to be integrated with other policies on employment, welfare, housing, health and other areas of life.

These should be linked into a strategic framework rather than operating in isolation from each other:

> *Policies which concentrate on widening access are likely to have limited impact unless they are integrated with wider, well-resourced strategies to combat poverty and social exclusion.* (Coffield 2000c)

Reform of the benefit system

A good example of articulation between different policy areas would be reform of the Benefit system to make it easier for unemployed people to engage in structured learning. The 16-hour rule applied to people on Job Seekers' Allowance is irreconcilable with the objective of encouraging lifelong learning. According to an analysis, 1,256 people had their benefit denied in the first half-year to September 2000 because they were suspected of undertaking a course of more than 16 guided learning hours. Of these only 487 were eventually confirmed as ineligible, and a further 57 of these won their benefit on appeal (*Working Brief*, 2001a). The punitive aspect of the rule inevitably has the effect of deterring people from engaging in education:

> *the emphasis on work as the principal means of dealing with poverty (...) forces the Benefit system into a disciplinary mode of operation that many disadvantaged people experience as oppressive, and consequently resist or withdraw from. (...) Sometimes these experiences are likely to alienate them from the worlds of both education and training. Our study shows that people are wary of finding themselves under pressure to give up courses which they are enjoying because some kind of work is available, or alternatively completing a training course but with no job prospects at the end of it.* (Bowman et al, 2000: 42)

Other practical measures that could help to widen participation would be:

- Extension of some of the programmes and initiatives that have proved most effective in attracting people who would not usually approach a formal education provider (e.g. extension of the Adult and Community Learning Fund which has now been agreed).

- Extension of national campaigns for learning (such as Adult Learners' Week).
- Simplification of the qualifications framework and greater recognition by employers and the QCA of flexible accreditation schemes such as those developed within the Open College Networks.
- Development of more qualifications for adults. The needs of young people and adults are different and those who return to education later on in life need 'a proper and broad array of qualifications suitable for adults' (Sargant and Tuckett, 1997: 11).
- The introduction of a national credit framework with a unit-led system for recognition of achievement, as proposed in *Learning Works* (Kennedy, 1997). In Wales, the Credit and Qualification Framework project is developing a single system uniting all accreditation systems across post-16 learning through the currency of credit (Reynolds, 2001).
- Development of an accredited national training scheme for developing the skills needed to deliver appropriate learning in a community context (outreach skills, guidance skills, bridging informal and formal learning, etc). There is an urgent need to equip adult and further education staff with the multiple skills required in outreach and community development work.
- Provision of more face-to-face, community-based guidance. From the focus groups she conducted, Dinsdale (2001) concluded that educational guidance provision for adults was totally inadequate:

    It is unlikely that the people I spoke to would go along to colleges for this guidance and where formal agencies have been used it doesn't seem to have been successful, in that people felt 'pushed' in inappropriate directions. The guidance, like the courses, needs to be delivered locally by trusted and trained people. (p12)

- The imposition of a legal duty on television channels to provide educational programmes:

    in order to maximise participation among the widest range of participant groups there is a need for all terrestrial broadcasting channels to be charged with a legal obligation to secure a range of educative programming.(...) No state committed to the creation of a Learning Society can dodge its obligation. (Tuckett and Sargant, 1999: 66)

Changes to institutional practice

Many providers of education and training are already attracting a wider social cross section of learners through a range of strategies. However overall progress is still uneven and some post-16 institutions and centres have not yet achieved any meaningful change in their student profile.

Reflecting on past practice

Providers, like policy-makers, need to take on board and reflect on the lessons from past practice:

> *There are loads of lessons out there but they are very diffuse and the necessary connections aren't made. The evidence needs to be collected and collated. We need to stand back a little from it. A theme that runs through the whole widening participation debate is fear of theory or reflection. We're afraid of an intellectual process. Somehow this is seen as a betrayal of what you're supposed to be doing. It's all about practice. People out there in the field haven't picked up the challenge to reflect more. There isn't the space or doesn't seem to be the space. There needs to be a space to reflect more on what we've done and combine that with practice.* (Interviewee)

Practical measures

There are some relatively minor measures large education institutions could take to create a more welcoming and reassuring ambience for people who are not traditional learners. These include clearly signposting main entrances; providing a welcoming and comfortable reception area, and making sure that reception desks are staffed, and telephones answered, by persons with good communication skills and the knowledge to respond to queries.

Although these are very obvious requirements they are not always provided, especially in higher education institutions where one sometimes has to search long and hard for a main reception point which often turns out to be either deserted or so protected with barriers and security guards that it bears a greater resemblance to Fort Knox than to a site of learning. Some institutions are also very difficult to contact by telephone.

Staff appointments

Providers would achieve greater equality in their student intake if there were strategies to recruit tutors, development workers, and, indeed, managers, as well as administration and clerical workers, from the communities they need to engage more with.

More accurate targeting

Not all the groups currently targeted are the most educationally disadvantaged and institutions may need to revise their assumptions about the ones at whom they need to direct most efforts. This applies to all educational sectors:

Part-time students are predominately mature students, but they are not necessarily disadvantaged. The student profile is very close to that of younger students. Simply by expanding their intake of part-time students, therefore, universities will not be contributing to social inclusion policies. To achieve this they will need to target their part-time provision directly at disadvantaged groups. There is little evidence so far that this is happening. (Woodrow, 2000a: 16)

Investing in outreach

In many areas, outreach work is essential to attract the groups least likely to engage in organised learning activities but in order to be effective it requires managerial commitment and adequate resourcing.

The effectiveness of any widening participation initiative depends ultimately on the skills and personality of the workers and tutors concerned, the terms and conditions of their appointment, and the extent of management support, supervision and training they receive. The importance of people in encouraging wider participation should be recognised by giving appropriate status and conditions of appointment. Employing development workers on short-term and fractional contracts means that the amount that they can achieve will inevitably be limited.

Staff development

Given the range of skills required in order to widen participation successfully, staff development should be a priority. Appropriate training sessions could help managers and institution-based staff to benefit from the knowledge and the expertise of outreach staff in supporting the progression of new groups from community settings into a more formal educational environment.

Outreach workers can help institutional staff to understand the reasons for the under-representation of some groups and identify the different approaches that might encourage their participation. What works for one group will not necessarily work for another. Widening learner intake involves a diversity of approaches recognising that different strategies suit different circumstances.

Some education institutions currently undertaking widening participation projects have no history of providing for under-represented groups. Consequently staff have little or no knowledge of the teaching and delivery approaches that will be most appropriate and effective with these groups. Staff development activities should therefore be designed to help part-time and full-time staff work more effectively with a wider range of learners:

It is clear that if more people, with more diverse needs and in a wider variety of settings are going to be participating in learning at different stages of their lives, then the type of pedagogy that is currently employed is unlikely to be equal to the task. (Hodgson and Spours, 1999: 21)

Provision of routes between informal and formal learning

To encourage people to engage in formal learning there need to be some routes between informal community-based learning and formal learning. Without articulation between informal and formal education, between community learning and further education, and between further education and higher education, it is unlikely that many new learners will progress to higher levels of study:

> *Universities can only get at under-represented groups if there are progression routes and if colleges aren't proactive there are no pathways. There's a need for partnerships not just to encourage pathways but to encourage colleges into new ways of working. That's a long-term project. Many HEIs are finding this a problem.* (Interviewee)

Implicit in this is the need to make progression to mainstream easier and more attractive to groups with no tradition of post-compulsory learning.

Influencing the mainstream

To widen participation in the holistic way envisaged by Kennedy (1997) education institutions need to adjust their practices, procedures and curricula to the needs of new learner groups. To help new learners to adjust to organised learning environments it is important that the lessons from adult community learning are used to influence mainstream procedures and practices. This means building a bridge between informal and formal learning, without losing the flexibility and dynamism of the former in the process:

> *However valuable local community-based initiatives might be, projects are not going to be sufficient on their own {to widen participation}. Lessons of {widening participation projects} need to be built into mainstream policies and organisational cultures.* (Mayo and Collymore, 2000: 156)

> *In moving from the margins to the mainstream, there can be as much loss as gain. The danger is that in the process all that was distinctive about the provision may be lost, including the all-important questions about purpose, participation and power.* (Whaley, 2000: 138)

To encourage sustained and successful participation, mainstream providers should recognise, value and integrate the different knowledge, perceptions and experience that new learners bring:

In terms of educational entitlement individuals have been manipulated into accepting or believing that different social groups have certain kinds of educational rights. When new discourses eventually invite these social groups to claim learning for themselves it is usually at the denial of their social or cultural identity – producing confused and fragmented participation rates amongst the excluded as they struggle to reposition themselves amid the changing discourses of inclusion. Measures to address new learning opportunities must recognise that new rationalities for participation need to overcome the more embedded arguments of past power relations and must acknowledge people's identities as an integral aspect of learning. (Preece, 2000: 3-4)

Supporting learners

Widening participation strategies will only succeed if they include measures to ensure that people not only access organised learning opportunities but also become successful learners. People with little prior experience of post-compulsory learning need to be supported throughout the learning process and their progress and achievements should, therefore, be monitored. FEFC (2000a), however, found that few colleges record data relating to achievements in non-accredited learning and few collect data relating to students' broader achievements when they are on accredited programmes.

If there is a genuine commitment to widening participation, institutions need to monitor their retention, achievement and progression rates and develop strategies to address any persistent patterns of under-achievement among learners from particular backgrounds (Haque, 2001).

Research gaps

There are still some gaps in our knowledge of what will bring about wider participation, and a number of uncharted areas where research might help policy-makers and practitioners to gain a better understanding of adult learning and participation patterns. Useful research might include:

- Long-term impact studies to find out what kind of interventions are most effective and why.
- Investigations of the extent and nature of the informal learning people engage in and how this can be recognised, built on and maximised.
- Longitudinal investigations into the inter-generational impact of adult learning, for example, the effect of adult participation on staying-on rates.
- An examination of the impact of different financial incentives and funding models on access, completion and progression.

- An investigation into the ways in which colleges are using Access funds to support wider participation and particular curriculum strategies, and which parts of Access funds have proved to be the most effective interventions.
- An examination of the impact of transport conditions and costs on participation.
- Research into the respective influence of factors such as compulsion, new funding and provision initiatives, personal motivation and the influence of other people in encouraging people to return to learning.
- An examination of ways of identifying and recording the outcomes of non-accredited programmes, especially value-added, among new groups of learners.
- Impact studies of the effectiveness of small projects and initiatives in widening participation:

  Most of the evidence that exists tends to cover the participation and reach of the schemes, the numbers involved etc, and stakeholder perceptions. There is a particular dearth of data which links the intervention to the desired outcome i.e., a sustained participation in learning activities. This is not uncommon and in part reflects a policy formation culture where being seen to be doing something (preferably innovative) is as important if not more important than achieving success. However, it also reflects the difficulties inherent in summative evaluations including: distinguishing between the range of factors which influence the outcomes of interventions; the difficulty in determining the counter-factoral (i.e., what would have happened without the intervention), and the time it takes to see whether a policy is effective or not. (Howard, 2001: 2)

- An investigation of ways of encouraging learning in small and immediate enterprises (SMEs).
- An investigation into the kinds of methodologies that are being used in researching widening participation.

There is also a need to connect research and policy to a greater degree than happened during the last decade:

There's a gap between research and political activism – between those in the research community in the field and those engaged in campaigning about policy and policy implementation: not enough dialogue between them. There is interesting writing going on but a gap between this and people in the front line dealing with government. This may be due to a reluctance to grapple on the one hand with some of the difficult lessons of research, and on the other with the messy business of policy. Ironically there was more closeness during the Tory period when people were embattled. It's because of the more opportunity-focused environment. The advent of New Labour gave opportunities for policy development and acting in open domain that hadn't been possible for ages and this opened up the gap. How we structure intellectual work with policy development is a problem which is much wider than just in education. (Interviewee)

* * *

The various measures suggested in this chapter, together with research into the areas listed, could help to bring about a more equitable post-16 system. Because of the diversity of adults and their circumstances, however, there can be no single or definitive solution to widening participation and it has to be worked at on a number of fronts. There are, though, certain enduring characteristics of British social and educational culture which ensure that, whatever national or institutional steps are taken, significant changes are unlikely to occur in the short-term. These include:

> *an obsession with perpetuating hierarchies; a continuing focus on selection; the tolerance of social pecking orders based on class and educational attainment – all of these are deeply part of the UK culture that must be shifted.* (Howard, 2001: 3)

Such a shift will only take place in the long-term and maybe only after a generation. One can only hope, therefore, that the lack of an immediate and visible impact on participation trends will not result in the goal of widening participation ending up in the crowded graveyard of so many previous policy thrusts.

Chapter 9

Final thoughts

The strong policy emphasis that has been put on widening participation in recent years is an acknowledgement that post-compulsory education and training provision still benefits too narrow a segment of the population. Whereas the overall number of adult participants in organised learning has grown over the last decade, their social composition has remained stubbornly resistant to change.

Many of the barriers and constraints that prevent people for engaging in education are the same as they were when I conducted research into adult participation at the end of the 1980s. However, most of the measures introduced to overcome these have targeted the practical obstacles – those related to time, costs and accessibility – rather than the dispositional and attitudinal ones which are harder to shift. For reasons that are deeply embedded in our national culture, there remains a suspicion and apprehension about education among many of those who engage in it least. There is still a widespread tendency to equate all forms of learning with formal compulsory education and to perceive education in general as the preserve of an exclusive and more affluent segment of the population. Yet there is a lingering tendency in policy to attribute non-participation more to individual apathy or lack of motivation than to the failure of the education and training system to be relevant and attractive to a large proportion of the adult population. As Gorard (2000b: 190) has observed, 'if nearly a third of the population does not wish to take part after formal schooling it is just possible that the problem lies in the provision and not in the non-participants'. Moreover, economic and policy factors have played a large part, over the last decade, in shaping both the extent and nature of learning opportunities and the extent and nature of adult participation.

Looking back over the last ten years, it can be seen that policy measures and related funding regimes have exerted a sometimes contradictory push and pull effect on adult learning patterns. The successive structural and funding changes imposed on the post-16 system, albeit often introduced with the aims of simplification and increasing demand for learning, have in some respects acted as inhibitors to participation and helped to maintain the traditional middle-class learner profile. In spite of the drive towards lifelong learning, the recent history of widening participation has been one of stop-go and ending up virtually where we started.

The main reasons for this, as explored in the previous chapters, include the long decline in public funding for informal and non-accredited community-based learning; over-reliance on short-term and small-scale measures to engage under-represented groups; the Schedule 2/Non-Schedule 2 curriculum divide and the obsession with measurement of outcomes such as qualifications and 'progression'.

In the last five years there has been a strong policy concern with opening up learning opportunities to the groups and communities least represented in organised provision. This has led to numerous positive policy measures and initiatives – the repeal of Schedule 2; the introduction of postcode funding mechanisms in further and higher education; widening participation project funding; increased finance for local authority services; new funding streams for adult learning; financial incentives to learn; a range of ICT initiatives, and a commitment to giving local people a greater say in determining the kind of opportunities that are provided. All of these reflect a genuine intention to make organised learning more accessible and attractive to those who currently take least advantage of it. The new measures have enabled new partnerships to emerge and new groups to participate in supported learning activities. Take-up of Individual Learning Accounts (ILAs) (before their suspension in October 2001) exceeded expectations; a network of new learning centres has been established and the Learning and Skills Council has launched a number of initiatives designed to widen participation in learning such as the 'bite-sized' course campaign. The Learning and Skills Councils will also, hopefully, eliminate some of the wide geographical disparities that have long characterised the distribution of adult learning opportunities.

The weaknesses of current measures

Despite their number and range, however, current measures are probably unlikely to achieve the significantly increased demand for learning that is the goal of Government. As suggested in Chapter 8, in order to achieve this we will need to go somewhat further than the string of laudable initiatives that has been launched since 1997. Although all of these should have a positive impact, the extent to which they will transform the traditional participant typology is questionable. This is partly because of the limitations and contradictions in policy itemised in Chapter 7 which have cancelled out many of the gains.

The Social Exclusion Unit report *Bringing Britain Together* (1999) cited several reasons why there had been no progress in neighbourhood renewal in previous years

– too many initiatives were short-term and unconnected and top-down rather than locally-inspired and -managed; agencies had been working separately rather than collaboratively; too much attention had been paid to infrastructures and too little to people; policies were not based on evidence and policy and funding measures were too short-term. All of these judgments could be applied to educational policy over the last decade and there is a danger that some of the same mistakes could be made again.

First, there is still too great a reliance on what Ecclestone (2001) has described as a 'sticking plaster' approach to widening participation – unconnected, short-term pilot initiatives or special measures, many of which are based on notions of relative disadvantage and require communities to compete for a share of resources. The new funding initiative that probably has the most potential for widening participation – the Adult and Community Learning Fund – has so far been too limited and small-scale to achieve anything more than small local changes. There is an urgent need for the battery of widening participation strategies to be brought together into one broad, over-arching strategy.

Second, the main emphasis in current post-16 policy is still on formal education. Policies are still concerned mainly with individual, linear learning trajectories and pay little attention to the collective and shared learning in which such trajectories often originate. The scale and significance of informal learning has yet to be recognised.

There is also a continuing and obsessive stress on 'what can be measured, weighed and marked' (Tuckett, 2001a). Despite recognition in policy documents of the role and value of non-accredited programmes that respond to community interests and needs, qualifications and educational progression remain the priority. Non-accredited provision tends to be seen only as a progression route although much non-accredited learning is engaged in and valued for itself:

> *It would be unfortunate and indeed ironic given the declared intentions of the Government if the LSC should repeat some of the mistakes arising from the 1992 Act by subscribing to the assumption that non-accredited learning necessarily functions as the 'first step' in a progression ladder taking the learner inexorably onwards and upwards. Learner purpose is far more complex and unpredictable.* (Turner, 2001: 7)

There can be significant spin-offs from less formal, non-accredited learning that are more valuable than vertical progression for individuals. There can be an impact on families (their expectations and aspirations); on children (their school performance and perception of the value of learning); and on local communities (an increase in community involvement and activism) – although the extent of the impact may in all cases be hard to quantify.

It is ironic in view of the political emphasis on widening participation that the part of the educational spectrum most likely to achieve that aim – informal, non-accredited, adult learning activities – is the one that continues to receive the least political and financial support:

> *Time and time again the most promising lifelong learning initiatives on the margins of education and employment have suffered the chronic insecurity of under-funding. (Nash, 1999)*

> *How can you embed when you only have access to short-term funding which requires bidding, bidding, bidding?* (Informant)

It is hard to disagree, therefore, with Johnston's judgment that the current approach to lifelong learning is: 'over-individualised, over-regulated and over dependent on access to the formal education system' (2000: 177). Moreover, the word 'lifelong' is probably a misnomer since in the corporate plan for the Learning and Skills Council, priority has been unequivocally given to younger adults aged 16-18. All that is proposed for adults is 'reasonable' provision – a term that is just as vague as 'adequate' was in the 1990s. No policies are advocated for older (50+) learners whose learning needs continue to be ignored.

Another weakness in current policy is the continuing failure to introduce measures to persuade employers to provide more learning opportunities for the groups of workers who have traditionally been most excluded – manual workers in unskilled occupations, those working in smaller firms, part-time and temporary workers, older workers.

Ignoring lessons of the past

There has also been a failure to draw on the lessons of the past. A wealth of existing evidence on working with under-represented groups has been neglected which has resulted in considerable time and resources being spent on research and national enquiries that have rediscovered much of what has long been known: *'We've been researched to death. When is something going to happen?'* (Member of a local community to interviewee)

The tendency to *'start again from scratch and reinvent the policy wheel each decade'* (Sargant and Tuckett, 1997) means that past successes are never built on. Thus a steady and cumulative move towards wider participation cannot be accomplished and many feel that recent policy measures designed to encourage wider participation have been too piecemeal, too swift and too uninformed:

> *A barrage of sometimes unconnected initiatives won't achieve widening participation.* (Interviewee)

Typically what service planners are doing is trying to meet too many priorities and too many target groups. So many attempts to engage people are hit and miss. (Interviewee)

What we may be learning is that institutional reform, endless initiatives and rhetoric about lifelong learning do not guarantee improved outcomes. (Robinson, 2000)

It is also widely felt that expectations of current measures are too high and do not take account of the time it takes to achieve significant cultural change:

There's almost too much being loaded onto lifelong learning and widening participation but they won't deliver short-term pay-offs. This could lead to abandonment and possible discrediting. (Interviewee)

People involved in the widening participation agenda are in too much of a hurry. It requires at least two generations to shift the culture. (Interviewee)

Too much, in particular, is expected of current 'flagship' initiatives, especially UfI. There is a naïve faith in the ability of ICT-based approaches to engage the most under-represented groups which is not widely shared by practitioners:

It is likely that a sober assessment of the UfI and related initiatives (...) will reveal their relative powerlessness to attract and retain precisely those adults who are most in need of them, and on whose needs the rhetorical appeal of such programmes is partly founded. (Gorard, 2000b: 191)

Many feel that too much is expected from lifelong learning in general, and that it is regarded by politicians as:

the magic key to solving everything from low self-esteem, Alzheimer's disease, poor housing, fragmented communities to lack of civic pride. (Ecclestone, 2000)

However, as Robinson (2000) warns:

We must be careful not to claim too much for learning. Advocacy of lifelong learning is based on the assertion that all learning will pay off in terms of both personal fulfilment and wider economic outcomes. If this is true, it is hard to see why people are not banging on the doors of our learning institutions.

Policy assumptions

Looking at current policy as a whole, some of the assumptions on which it is based are questionable and this, perhaps more than anything, may be why any significant changes in participation patterns may not be easily achieved.

A major assumption that needs to be challenged is that non-participation in organised learning is largely due to the attitudes and inadequacies of individuals. The language used in some recent policy documents and survey reports implies that there is something wrong with people who do not habitually engage in education and training. The report of the DfEE *Pathways in Adult Learning* survey (La Valle and Finch, 1999), for example, refers to 'long-term non learners' as 'high risk groups' and points to the need to change 'behaviour and attitudes at an individual level'. There is a tinge of condescension in this as it suggests that people are wilfully not engaging in something that will automatically be good for them (another questionable assumption). It also ignores the fact that the people so described may be engaging in a range of learning activities which are relevant and useful to them but which do not fall into the categories of taught and self-directed learning used in the survey.

Unhelpful stereotypes of 'non-learners' abound in recent reports. It has become the norm to equate non-participation with notions of disadvantage and deficiency.

As a result, much of what is now seen as widening participation activity is remedial or compensatory in nature, although this focus will not necessarily change adult participation patterns:

> *A relentless diet of basic skills won't widen participation'* (Interviewee)

> *If the LSC's marketing of learning is targeted too obviously towards compensatory programmes, this will simply reinforce the stultifying perception that learning is irrelevant to mainstream adult life'.* (Wilkins, 2001)

But because people are not engaging in education and training does not automatically mean that they are 'deprived'; nor does it mean that they inevitably have poor literacy and numeracy skills:

> *Once we let these {negative} labels take hold, we view people from 'non-traditional' groups who do not venture through the doors of institutions as in need of 'help'. We should see them as people with diverse needs, abilities and aspirations but who might be "hard to reach". Increasingly it seems that anyone who doesn't participate in learning must be 'dejected' and 'disaffected'.* (Ecclestone, 2000)

We also need to challenge the assumption underlying policy discourses on lifelong learning that the people who do not engage in structured learning have an obligation to conform to a standard, middle-class life-style and set of values: in other words, as one practitioner put it, we are asking everybody to change except ourselves:

> *Debates about widening participation reflect those in the 1960s about race relations, i.e. how to bring different cultures into mainstream. We're about bringing people into 'our' system, never questioning the legitimacy and validity of that system.* (Interviewee)

The implication here is that everyone has access to the same educational and employment opportunities and that all that is needed is for people to overcome their inertia. This ignores the huge regional and local disparities in the availability of jobs and education and training opportunities and the common research finding that people's perceptions of the 'opportunities' available to them frequently do not coincide with the perceptions of policy-makers.

There is also a lack of appreciation of the multiple constraints faced by many people and the hurdles they need to overcome in order to participate on an equal footing with others in education and the labour market:

> *An unfortunate feature of government is the assumption it makes that everybody can be dealt with in the same fashion in terms of attempting to lever them into the labour force, education or training system. The reality of living at the margins of society in terms of income, security, status, other networks, obligations and responsibilities, may make it very difficult for people to take up what are viewed in policy terms as normal and legitimate opportunities.* (Bowman *et al*, 2000: 41-42).

Cultural disparities

Thus simply opening up education institutions to new learners through mechanisms such as postcode targeting (albeit a welcome measure) is not enough to widen participation among the most disadvantaged groups to any significant degree. Foreshadowing Bourdieu's (1977) arguments, Midwinter (1971) observed 30 years ago that:

> *equality of opportunity without equality of circumstances is largely a sham. (...) As it stands the educational system offers the same product to all. This is in trite terms, a ladder for all to climb, but as only a few obviously can reach the top, it is in part an education for frustration (...) The rules of the game are indubitably the same for everyone; it's just that some of the participants are nobbled.* (p2)

This applies as much to adults as to working-class children adjusting to a middle-class education culture. Adults moving into an unfamiliar learning environment often experience discomfort and a sense of disorientation. However, the difficulties of moving away from familiar cultural reference points are routinely underestimated or ignored. Class divisions in post-compulsory education and training are maintained by opening some doors (making provision and institutions more accessible) but leaving others shut (not providing the necessary supports for learners). The mutual support and encouragement that provide the glue and stimulus in so many successful informal learning groups are not always replicated in more formal education environments and the range of practical supports that many people need in order to engage successfully in structured learning may not be available. Notwithstanding all the changes that have been imposed on the post-compulsory sector in the last ten years (which, to quote Stephen Ball's (1990) judgment on the policies of the 1980s, have largely 'outrun the development of relevant analysis and conceptualisation' (p7)), many education and training institutions have still not made the necessary changes and adjustments to accommodate a greater diversity of learners.

This is partly because of an innate conservatism that pervades educational policy and practice. As Smyth (1998) has found in Ireland, there is 'serious ideological and systemic resistance, in terms of policy development and state funding mechanisms, as well as within academic institutions, to innovation in almost any sphere'. This reflects a wider conservatism within society as a whole ('the forces of tradition are so entrenched in this society that change will never gain consensus' (Interviewee) and underlies the ambivalence towards wider participation among some policy-makers, institutional managers and public figures who fear that it may lower standards.

Yet, as Whaley (2000:138) points out, 'diversity can coexist with quality; rigour with innovation, standards with equivalence' and not all analysts think there should be a contradiction between widening participation and academic standards (Ward and Steele, 1999). Moreover, evidence suggests that retention and achievement rates may be related more to inequalities in class, gender and ethnicity than to individual ability or commitment (Utley, 2001). As I have argued elsewhere:

> *It is an indication of our ambivalence towards people who are educationally and socially disadvantaged, that when they do engage successfully in formal learning and aspire to higher qualification levels, their incursion into a world so long and so firmly dominated by the middle classes is greeted with widespread alarm. Having previously been held responsible for their lack of educational participation and progress, new groups who enter further and higher education by 'non-standard' routes are blamed for lowering and devaluing standards. This is like inviting people to a private club but when they get there, informing them that it is for members only. In the first year of the new Millennium, there is still a 'class' ceiling in our education and training system that is waiting to be smashed.* (McGivney, 2001: 51)

Unless the proper supports are in place for new learners, widening participation is bound to have an impact on levels of achievement and completion:

> *What will really achieve the widening participation agenda is if people can perform in the established (education) terrain as well as the groups who always have participated.* (Interviewee)

Education institutions, however, feel pulled in opposing directions. On the one hand they are being encouraged to admit a wider mix of learners; on the other they are expected to meet stringent standards to do with retention and achievement and, in the case of higher education, research excellence. The respective weight attached to these competing considerations is illustrated by the fact that higher education institutions are rewarded far less for efforts to widen participation than for quality research. Can it be accidental that some of the institutions which have made the greatest efforts to broaden their pool of learners have run into financial difficulties? As Kennedy (1997) has pointed out, attracting and keeping those for whom learning is a daunting experience is both hard work and financially unrewarding.

Given some of the financial risks involved for publicly-funded providers, it is perhaps not surprising that many of the initiatives that have been most successful in widening participation have either functioned outside the education system altogether or have been so short-term and insecurely funded that their impact has been limited.

All of this suggests that the culture shift among non-participants so often called for in policy documents, needs also to occur at policy and provider level:

> *The culture change that is needed is at least as much a culture change for the supply-side: policy-makers, funders, providers and teachers. Perhaps we are the 'hard-to-reach' for those who do not connect with the learning system.* (Howard, 2001:2)

Such a shift will require those who make educational policy to embrace a much wider and more comprehensive view of learning than is currently the case and to retreat from the all-pervasive instrumentalism that has bedevilled adult learning for nearly two decades.

Continuing supremacy of instrumental objectives

The focus on the link between education and employment has had a powerful impact on the supply and funding of learning opportunities over the last decade and the ultimate goal of lifelong learning is still seen as greater employability and jobs. Government support for adult learning therefore often has some restrictions attached: for example, tax relief and Individual Learning Accounts have been available only for specific types of course.

The continuation of this emphasis in current policy is something that many analysts view with dismay (see, for example, Coffield, 1999; Elliott, 1999; Hunt, 1999; Martin,1999). The emphasis on learning to increase 'employability' takes little account of the large number of people excluded from the labour market because of age, sickness, family responsibilities or disability; little account of the competing pressures of work and family commitments; and no account at all of the conspicuous failure of a succession of government work-related schemes to improve the life-chances of long-term unemployed people. It suggests that jobless individuals are outside the labour market as a result of their lack of skills, which is insulting to those booted prematurely out of work because of industrial decline, downsizing or ageism. It consolidates the shift of power to employers that occurred during the Conservative years by implying that individuals are wholly responsible for their success or failure in the labour market, regardless of the dearth of jobs, the insecure nature of many jobs and the hire-and-fire practices of employers however unfair or discriminatory these might be. Moreover, the assumption that education or training will automatically lead to employment is questionable. Although higher achievement levels can make a significant difference to the chances of young people without qualifications and poor basic skills, many adults over 25 who have increased their qualification levels have not succeeded in finding work commensurate with the qualifications gained. Mature graduates, for example, are less successful in finding employment than younger students.

The related assumption that employment will eliminate social exclusion is also questionable. As the labour market is itself highly stratified and unequal, it is unlikely that the gap between the affluent and the poor will be significantly bridged by forcing more people into low-paid and precarious employment:

> *I've never seen any research on whether the benefits of moving people through the system into work (assuming this is a key objective) lead to a happier or better life. Is it the right job?* (Interviewee)

Thus the argument that the solution to exclusion is employment just does not hold up. Moreover, the premise on which arguments for lifelong learning are based may be a false one. Although the main selling point for lifelong learning is that it will lead to improved job opportunities and, therefore, to greater personal prosperity, those already in work (especially at higher employment levels) are far more likely to engage in education or training than those who are not. Labour market position is still a key determinant of participation in learning (La Valle and Finch, 1999). In other words, employment seems to lead to adult engagement in learning rather than *vice versa*.

There is also a danger that the overly-strong instrumental emphasis in policy will skew the nature of provision and result in curricular and cultural imbalances by fostering a situation in which post-16 programmes of study are primarily supported and valued for their relation to the job market. This again is based on a false premise, as pointed out by O'Rourke (1995):

> *The drive to match education and training to the needs of industry is a double deception: the economy isn't damaged by degrees in the humanities and won't be saved by MBAs but the drive to pretend it will limits many students' choice of study on the spurious grounds that it will help them find employment.* (p120)

The salience of employment-related reasons for entering organised learning is hardly surprising given the emphasis placed on vocational education and training by successive governments and the fact that for many people, health and well-being are tied in with work. Nevertheless it could render some of the other goals of lifelong learning difficult to achieve:

> *The learners' view, and that of many employers, (…) is one which identifies lifelong learning as being 'job focused', not about benefits to the community or society and certainly not part of the current discussions about the role of lifelong learning in developing the nature of 'citizenship'.* (Atkin, 2000: 262)

To be fair, the UK is not unique in this respect. A UNESCO transnational project involving Canada, the Netherlands, Poland, Sweden, Switzerland, USA and the Canary Islands (Belanger and Valdivielso (eds), 1997) showed that, despite international acceptance of a broad and comprehensive understanding of lifelong learning, work-related learning had become the dominant form of adult education in all participating countries and was growing in importance at the same time that 'the parallel steady decline in jobs and massive downsizing of the workforce constitutes an anti-learning enterprise' (p 165). However, as pointed out in the chapter on the United States, work is not the whole of life. The author of this chapter quotes an educator's exasperated reaction to US legislation on literacy: 'Work! Work! Work! And not a single word about human dignity!' (Valentine, 1999: 108).

Even accepting the imperative to raise national skill levels, the instrumental emphasis in educational policy is probably unnecessary. There is ample evidence that 'employability' (if one must use such an ugly term) can be achieved by a diversity of learning routes. As argued earlier, the learning that flows from membership of voluntary organisations, from social action and protest, from active involvement in local communities and from engagement in a collective concern or enterprise frequently leads to the acquisition of a range of practical skills as well as the 'key' skills that are ostensibly sought by employers, although none of these activities are usually entered into with employment or employability as an aim. A 'clear conclusion' from the OECD (1999) study on overcoming exclusion through adult learning was that:

> *lifelong learning policies which focus primarily on jobs are castles built on sand. Those that support existing networks and address wider social issues are most likely to bolster employment long- term.* (Nash 1999)

Closing the skills gap and helping people to gain the knowledge, skills and competencies necessary to help them gain and stay in employment are essential roles of education and training but should they be the central aim? As stated in the OECD study (1999), the UK needs:

to understand social exclusion more clearly in terms other than the job market.

{It} has concentrated almost exclusively on issues of economic exclusion over the past two decades. The importance of investment in social capital and the concerns of the wider community have been neglected and at cost, not only to those individuals who have been marginalised through unemployment but to whole neighbourhoods. (pp 16 and 172)

However, it is hard to convince policy-makers that 'the primary purpose of education should not be the living that students will earn but the life they will lead' (Halsey *et al*, 1997). There is a lingering and deep-seated conviction that it is not worth investing public money in adult education unless it is to be undertaken for utilitarian purposes. This kind of thinking is found at every level of policy. Some members of local councils continue to perceive adult learning that is not employment-related as a self-indulgent and even frivolous leisure pursuit. While such attitudes persist it will be difficult to create the learning society that is the ostensible goal of government. If we genuinely want to help people to participate in learning, however, then the Local Learning and Skills Councils will need to look beyond economic and employment concerns. As stated in the NIACE (1999) response to the White Paper *Learning to Succeed*, lifelong learning needs to be driven by social as well as economic imperatives. Now that there is a new structure in place for the planning and funding of post-16 provision, it is time perhaps to remind the people involved of the words of the *Russell Report* published nearly 30 years ago:

the value of adult education is not solely to be measured by direct increases in earning power or productive capacity or by any other materialistic yardstick, but by the quality of life it inspires in the individual and generates for the community at large. (Russell, 1973: XI)

What does widening participation mean?

Revisiting Russell provides an opportunity to think about what widening participation really means or what it *should* mean. It should not just be about individual opportunities to acquire qualifications and jobs: it should be about building community capacity and producing collective social change. It should not just be about encouraging people without qualifications or with poor basic skills to remedy their perceived 'deficiencies': it should be about offering opportunities to the large numbers of people in our society who because of poverty and structural exclusion have had access to few of the advantages and resources available to more affluent groups. Efforts to widen participation should therefore aim to raise aspirations among those whose experience and background have provided them with very limited hopes and expectations. In other words, we need to face the barriers of social class head-on although this is:

> *deeply unpopular because it implies conflict, barriers, different groups competing against each other for limited resources and opportunities. It requires moral and political judgements to be made about fairness and social worth.* (Shaw *et al*, 2000: 5)

Acknowledgement of the critical impact of social class on participation requires us to see exclusion from education not in isolation but as part of a wider structural exclusion process. Educational disadvantage is inextricably linked with other forms of disadvantage, therefore attempts to widen participation in education should be integrated with social and economic policy and measures to improve housing, health, welfare and job opportunities:

> *Whatever our belief in the power of learning, it is still more likely in the short term that fuller participation will emerge as a result of a less polarised society than that a fairer society will emerge as a result of fuller participation in adult learning.* (Gorard, 2000b: 191)

The challenge for government is therefore to integrate the social inclusion and the economic agendas. These should not be mutually exclusive. Widening participation also requires a much wider approach than just increasing demand for the forms of education and training that already exist: 'promoting learning is a broader issue than flogging courses' (Interviewee). It should also go beyond area-based initiatives and target-setting and involve a comprehensive attempt to improve learning opportunities for *all* adults. To restate one of the conclusions of *Education's for Other People*,

> *The arguments for widening access should not be polarised into either traditional provision or work with new groups, but should make the case for a more flexible, multi-targeted service, operating from the recognition that the community is composed of different groups with equally valid learning interests and requirements.* (McGivney, 1990: 176)

Only a couple of years ago, these arguments seemed to have been accepted but there are now signs of some retrenchment.

Can wider participation be achieved?

As Chapter 8 has argued, there are some practical measures that would encourage more people to engage in organised learning: greater parity between government spending on adults and spending on the 16-18 cohort; longer-term policies and funding strategies that will allow providers to innovate, take risks and develop sustained work with excluded groups; the introduction of a financial entitlement up the Level 3 for all adults; initiatives in institutions that go beyond a concern with access and involve changes to mainstream procedures, practice and curricula; support for face-to-face guidance and outreach work; adequate rewards for grassroots practitioners (outreach workers, guidance workers, community education workers and tutors); – the hugely important role of learning intermediaries needs to be recognsed and resourced; and a statutory right for all workers to paid educational leave.

In addition to these, a 'more regulatory and less voluntarist approach to the labour market' (Hodgson and Spours, 1999: 6) would also contribute significantly to wider participation. It is odd that the policy emphasis on people making themselves more employable and adaptable to changes in the labour market is not paralleled by a similar stress on the need for employers to change and adapt and provide training opportunties for the whole workforce incuding part-time workers and those over 50.

The principal need, however, is for a broader notion of learning as something that is conducted for social and family reasons and for personal development, as well as for instrumental reasons, 'We mustn't forget the importance of learning for pleasure, for stimulation, for passion, for play' (Informant).

A person interviewed for this study referred to a fragment of David Bluckett's Preface to *The Learning Age* that has been 'untouched' in policy:

> *people's ability to express themselves culturally; people making culture. I'm sure we need to remake those connections between the arts as an expression of popular understanding. The result of that could have all sorts of impact on the employment agenda, or on the Literacy Campaign.*

An important question, therefore, is whether the operational definition of learning adopted by the LSC will acknowledge the diversity and creativity of provision needed to address the social imbalances in participation and enable providers of adult and community learning to deliver a varied, flexible and responsive programme of opportunities for adults:

> *We need to get people reflecting on and learning from their experience, people being able to make sense of their lives and gain control of their lives. This is very important. To create a learning culture we need to offer loosely structured opportunities that can be delivered in all sorts of ways. We need to provide for individuals who don't have instrumental aims but who may be interested in learning for its own sake or self-development.*
> (Interviewee)

Finally, learning cannot be divorced from the overall context of people's lives. To achieve a culture of lifelong learning, therefore, will require recognition of and support for learning that does *not* involve a formal course or programme of study but which is generated by and connected to people's everyday experience. In areas where rates of participation in formal learning are low it is possible to find that many adults are involved in a rich diversity of informal learning activities related to personal and local interests, priorities and concerns. More adult learning takes place within *non*-educational activities and environments – family life, community action, membership of clubs, groups or voluntary organisations, development of leisure interests – than in dedicated educational centres and institutions. This dimension of learning – which has long been neglected in policy and research – is the key to lifelong learning in disadvantaged communities.

There will not be a single solution to under-participation in learning, but international research data indicate that centrally-driven policies and measures can make a significant difference. In Sweden, for example, the package of measures introduced in the 1970s – social benefits for adult learners, subsidies for outreach activities, group targeting and the introduction of an Educational Leave Act – led to a more socially balanced participant profile than in any other part of the industrial world (Rubenson, 1999). However, it takes courage to introduce major shifts in priorities and resource allocation and there are as yet few signs that it will happen here.

A long-term project

It is clear that to change the traditional profile of participants in organised learning will be neither an easy nor a rapid process and even if all the measures mentioned in this study were implemented, there would still be a certain core of the population who would not participate. Not all of current non-participants will wish or need to engage in organised learning, and others will have considerable barriers to overcome before they are ready to embark on a learning path:

> *Issues go much deeper {than just getting people into organised education}; it's to do with schooling, society, general culture. Widening participation needs a more root and branch approach. If people only see the receiving end of widening participation they'll see some real jewels – individuals who come through adversity, whose commitment makes them shine. But we're not talking about this but about a whole cadre of society. The talented and the clever will always come through. Whole cultural shifts are much harder to achieve.* (Interviewee)

Social and cultural changes are more likely to occur in the long- than in the short-term and it may take up to a generation to change attitudes and behaviour. There are fears, however, that official interest in widening participation will wane if current policies do not produce rapid results:

I'm worried about the connection between wider participation and regeneration. I see this as a rather simplistic notion which, if it doesn't produce results in the short term (which it won't) may be rejected. Regeneration won't happen on this government's (and certainly the Treasury's) short time frame. (Interviewee)

Some feel that the 'fashion' for widening participation has already been superseded by other preoccupations such as the need to raise standards and to improve adult literacy and numeracy skills. However, participation has been widened before and can be again, given sufficient will and drive on the part of the key stakeholders. As Taylor (2000) reminds us, 30 years ago, despite resistance and the conservatism of the system, radical 'social purpose' adult educationists and feminists succeeded in challenging and significantly influencing adult education practices. If sufficient change does not come from the top, and if the new structures renege on their duty to listen to local people and respond to their learning preferences and needs, then there could be a resurgence of that creative energy.

References

Adult Learning Inspectorate, Employment Service, Learning and Skills Council and Ofsted (2001) *Raising standards in post-16 learning: self-assessment and development plans*, DfEE

Adults Learning (2000) 'The Increase in the Learning Divide', *Adults Learning*, June, pp13-14

Advisory Council for Adult and Continuing Education (1982) *Adults: their educational experience and needs*, Leicester: ACACE

Aldridge F (2000) *Fees survey 1999-2000: Indicators of fee levels charged to part-time adult students by local education authorities and colleges*, Leicester: NIACE

Aldridge F and Tuckett A (2001) *Winners and losers in an expanding system: the NIACE survey on adult participation in learning 2001*, Leicester: NIACE

Archer L and Ross A (2001) 'The Report falls short', *Times Higher Education Supplement*, 16 February, p16

Atkin C (2000) 'Lifelong learning – attitudes to practice in the rural context: a study using Bourdieu's perspective of habitus', *International Journal of Lifelong Education*, Vol 19 No.3 May-June, pp.253-64

Babchuk W and Courtney S (1995) 'Towards a sociology of participation in adult education programmes', *International Journal of Lifelong Education*, Vol 15 No 5, pp 391-404

Ball S J (1990) *Politics and policy-making in education: explorations in policy sociology*, London and New York: Routledge

Ball S J, Davies J, David M. and Reay D (2000) *ESRC funded HE choice project*, Draft paper 2. London: CPPR/King's College

Bamber J, Ducklin A and Tett L (2000) 'Working with contradictions in the struggle for access?' in Thompson J (ed) *Stretching the Academy*, Leicester: NIACE, pp 158-170

Baty P (2000) 'Poor fail to fill access places', *Times Higher Education Supplement*, 1 September, p 5

Beinart S and Smith P (1998) *The National Adult Learning Survey*, DfEE.

Belanger P and Valdivielso S (eds), (1997) *The emergence of learning societies: who participates in adult learning?* UNESCO Institute for Education: Pergamon.

Bell C (1999) 'Widening Participation: Policy divergences and convergences', *Update on Inclusion*, Issue No.2 Autumn pp 3-4

Bellis A, Clarke J and Ward J (1999) *Marginalised Voices: a survey of current practice on widening participation with minority ethnic communities*, UACE Occasional Paper No.24, Cambridge: UACE

Blackburn R M and Jarman J (1993) 'Changing inequalities in access to British universities', *Oxford Review of Education* pp 192, 197-216

Blunkett D (2000) *Learning and Skills Council Remit Letter*, DfEE

Bourdieu P (1977) 'Cultural Reproduction and Social Reproduction' in J Karabel and A.H Halsey (eds), *Power and Ideology in Education*, New York: Oxford University Press

———— (1993) *Sociology in question*, London: Sage

Bowman H, Burden T and Konrad J (2000), *Successful futures? Community views of adult education and training*, York: Joseph Rowntree Foundation/York Publishing Services

Boyer D (2001) 'Provider base set to change', *Working Brief*, April, pp 16-19

Boyson R (2000) 'Some ways of keeping the melting pot full of talent', *Times Higher Education Supplement*, 18 August, p 12

Brookfield S D (1986) *Understanding and facilitating adult learning*, Milton Keynes: Open University Press

Bynner J, Joshi H and Tsatsas M (2000) *Obstacles and opportunities on the route to adulthood: Evidence from rural and urban Britain*, London: Institute of Education Centre for Longitudinal Studies

Callender C (1999) *The hardship of learning: Students' income and expenditure and their impact on participation in FE*, Coventry: FEFC.

Callender C and Kemp M (2000) *Changing students' finances: income, expenditure and the take-up of student loans among full-time and part-time HE students in 1998-99*, DfEE Publications

Campaign for Learning/MORI, 1998, *Attitudes to learning*, London: Campaign for Learning

Cavanagh D (2000) 'Researching "inclusion": Reality and rhetoric; it's all in the curriculum approach', in Jackson A and Jones D (eds), *Papers from 30th annual conference of the Standing Conference on University Teaching and Research in the Education of Adults (SCUTREA)*, 3-5 July, University of Nottingham: Continuing Education Press, pp 35-40

Chisholm L (1998) 'From systems to networks: the reconstruction of youth transitions in Europe', in Heinz W (ed), *New passages between education and employment in a comparative life course perspective*, Cambridge: Cambridge University Press

Clarke A (2001) 'Closing the digital divide', *Adults Learning*, May, p 6

Clayton P (2000) 'Vocational Guidance and Inclusion in Lifelong Learning', *A global colloquium supporting lifelong learning, Open University, Festival of Lifelong Learning*, UEL, Open University and University of East London http://www.open.ac.uk/lifelong-learning

Clyne P (1972) *The disadvantaged adult: educational and social needs of minority groups*, Harlow: Longman

Coffield F (1999) *Breaking the consensus: Lifelong learning as social control*, Inaugural Lecture, Department of Education, University of Newcastle, 2 February.

———— (2000a) 'Introduction: a critical analysis of the concept of a learning society' in Coffield F (ed) *Differing visions of a learning society*, Vol 1, pp 1-11, Bristol: Policy Press

———— (2000b) 'The structure below the surface: Reassessing the significance of informal learning' in Coffield F (ed) *The Learning Society: The necessity of informal learning*, pp 1-31, Bristol: Policy Press

——— (2000c), 'Poverty won't be beaten so easily', *Times Educational Supplement* 8 December, p.34.

——— (2001) 'Castle of lifelong learning built on shifting sands of myth', *Times Educational Supplement: FE Focus*, 25 May, p 40

Committee of Vice-Chancellors and Principals (CVCP) (1998), *From elitism to inclusion: Good practice in widening participation in HE*, London: CVCP

Core Skills News (2000) *The story so far,* Birmingham: Core Skills Development Partnership

Crequer N (2000) 'No train, no gain, firms told', *Times Educational Supplement: FE Focus*, 6 October, p33

Davidson-Burnett G and Green S (1999) 'Widening Participation: The Role of UCAS Data', *Update on Inclusion*, Issue No.2 Autumn, pp11-12

Davies D (2001) Editorial, *Widening Participation and Lifelong Learning*, Vol 3 No1, pp2-3

Davies P and Ruddon T (2000) *Differential achievement: What does the ISR profile tell us?* London: LSDA

Department of Education and Science (DES) (1973) *Adult education: a plan for Development*, report by a Committee of Inquiry appointed by the Secretary of State for Education and Science under the chairmanship of Sir Lionel Russell, London: HMSO

Department of Education and Science and Employment Department (1991) *Education and Training for the 21st Century*

Department for Education and Employment (DfEE) (1995) *Lifetime Learning: A consultation document.*

——— (1996) *Lifetime Learning: A policy framework.*

——— (1998a) *New arrangements for effective student support in further education*: report of the FE student support advisory group

——— (1998b) *Adult and Community Learning Fund Prospectus*

——— (1999a) *Learning to succeed*

——— (1999b) *Skills for neighbourhood renewal: local solutions*, the final report of the Policy Action Team on Skills

——— (1999c) *Prospectus for Learning and Skills Council*

——— (2000a) *Tackling the adult skills gap: Upskilling adults and the role of workplace training*, third report of the National Skills Task Force

——— (2000b) *Skills for all: proposals for a national skills agenda*: final report of the National Skills Task Force

——— (2000c) *Guidance to Learning Partnerships*

Dinsdale J (2001) *Community voice: Focus group research with adult learners in Worcestershire, Worcester*: University College

Donnelly C (1997) 'Students and colleges frustrated by 21-hour rule', *Working Brief*, March, pp 10-14

Ecclestone K (2000) 'Held back by the taint of stereotypes', *Times Educational Supplement: FE Focus*, 9 June, pIV

——— (2001) 'Never mind the qualification – check the quality', *Times Educational Supplement: FE Focus*, 9 Feb, p 33

Edwards R (1997) *Changing places: Flexibility, lifelong learning and a learning society*, Routledge: London

——— (2000) 'Making spaces for lifelong learning: pedagogies of (dis)location' *Rising East*: Special Issue: Lifelong Learning and East London, Vol 4, No 2, pp 22-37

Edwards R, Raggatt P, Harrison R, McCollum A and Calder J (1998), Recent thinking in lifelong learning: A review of the literature, Research Report RR80, DfEE

Eldred J (2000) 'Adult literacy: understanding the past and reclaiming the future', *Adults Learning*, November, pp 10-11

Elliott J (1999) 'Whither vocationalism?' *Adults Learning*, September, pp 17-19

Elsdon K with Reynolds J and Stewart S (1995) *Learning in voluntary organisations: Citizenship, learning and change*, Leicester: NIACE

Employment Department (1993) *The strategy for skills and enterprise*

Farr M (2001) 'Home or Away? A Study of Distance Travelled to Higher Education 1994-1999', *Widening Participation and Lifelong Learning*, Vol 3 No 1, pp 17-19

Field J (1999) 'Participation under the magnifying glass', *Adults Learning*, 10 November, pp 11-13

———— (2000) *Lifelong learning and the new educational order*, Stoke on Trent: Trentham

———— (2001a) 'The Learning Age – is it just for youngsters or can adults join in too?', *Adults Learning*: Soapbox, March, pp 25-26

———— (2001b) 'Give us all a sniff of lifelong learning', *Times Education Supplement*, 25 May, p 38

Foley G (1999) *Learning in social action: A contribution to understanding informal education*, Leicester: NIACE

Forrester K and Payne J (1999) 'A sort of metamorphosis: the role of trade unions in widening participation in lifelong learning', *Widening Participation and Lifelong Learning*, Vol 1, No 2, pp 24-32

———— (2000) 'Will adult learning ever be popular?' in Jackson A and Jones D (eds), *Papers from 30th annual conference of the Standing Conference on University Teaching and Research in the Education of Adults* (SCUTREA), 3-5 July, University of Nottingham: Continuing Education Press, pp 99-105

Fox C (2001) 'ICT clearly now the brain has gone', *Times Education Supplement*, 25 May, p22

Fremeaux I (2000) 'Community and cultural policy: the Arts Worldwide Bangladeshi Festival', *Rising East*: the journal of East London Studies, Vol 3 No 3, pp 46-68

Fryer R H (1997) *Learning for the 21st Century*, First Report of the National Advisory Group for Continuing Education and Lifelong Learning, HMSO

Further Education Development Agency (FEDA) (1995) *Progression for adult learners from informal to qualification-bearing courses*, London: Further Education Development Agency

Further Education Funding Council (1996) *Inclusive Learning*, the report of the FEFC's Learning Difficulties and/or Disabilities Committee chaired by Professor John Tomlinson.

——— (1997) *How to widen participation: A guide to good practice*

——— (2000a) *Widening participation and raising standards*

——— (2000b) *Widening participation and raising standards: Colleges' case studies*

——— (2001) *Funding guidance on funding allocations 2100-2001*, Circular 01/15 March

Further Education Funding Council News (2000) No 63, December

Goddard A (2000a) 'An open door is not enough', *Times Higher Education Supplement*, 15 September, p 9

——— (2000b) 'Elite told to take more minorities', *Times Higher Education Supplement*, 13 October, p 4

——— (2001) 'Grants revive mature interest', *Times Higher Education Supplement*, 20 July, p 1

Gorard S (2000a) 'Robbing Peter to pay Paul: resolving the contradiction of lifelong learning', *A global colloquium supporting lifelong learning, Open University, Festival of Lifelong Learning*, UEL, Open University and University of East London http://www.open.ac.uk/lifelong-learning

——— (2000b) 'Adult participation in learning and the economic imperative: a critique of policy in Wales', *Studies in the Education of Adults*, Vol 32, No 2, October pp 181-94

Great Britain Committee on Higher Education (1963) *Higher Education*: report of the Committee appointed by the Prime Minister under the Chairmanship of Lord Robbins 1961-1963 ('The Robbins Report'), London: HMSO

Green F (1999) 'Training the Workers', in Gregg P and Wadsworth J (eds), *The state of working Britain*, Manchester: Manchester University Press

Greenwood M, Merton A and Taylor S (2000) *An evaluation of non-schedule 2 pilot projects*, London: LSDA

Grennan P (2000) 'Beyond Schedule 2', *College Research*, Winter, London: Learning and Skills Development Agency, p 32

Halsey A H (1998) 'Leagues Apart', *Times Higher Education Supplement*, 6 February, p 17

Halsey A H, Lauder H, Brown P, and Wells A S (1997) *Education: culture, economy and society*, Oxford: Oxford University Press

Haque Z (2001) 'Retention rates by social and ethnic group – implications for HEIs,' *Update on Inclusion*, Issue 3, Spring, pp 11-13

Hayes A (1999) *Making the future: Women students in the new further education*, Ph.D thesis, Centre for Educational Studies, University of London (unpublished)

Hemstedt A 'Family literacy and numeracy', *College Research*, Winter 2000, London: Learning and Skills Development Agency, pp 20-21

Herbert A and Callender C (1997) *The funding lottery: student financial support in FE and its impact on participation*, London: Policy Studies Institute

Higher Education Funding Council (England) (1996) Widening Access to Higher Education, Bristol: HEFCE

Hillage J and Aston J (2001) *Attracting new learners: a literature review*, Institute for Employment Studies/Learning and Skills Development Agency

Hillage J, Uden T, Aldridge F and Eccles J (2000), *Adult learning in England: a review*, NIACE/Institute for Employment Studies

Hodgson A and Spours K (1999) *New Labour's educational agenda: issues and policies for education and training from 14+*, London: Kogan Page

Hook, S (2001) 'Budget slashed for adult learning', *Times Education Supplement*, 20 April, p1

Howard U (2001) *Stimulating demand for learning: an ideas paper on attracting new learners*, London: Learning and Skills Development Agency

Hoy J, Kumrai R and Webb, S (2000), 'Practitioner research with a difference: widening participation projects', in Jackson A and Jones D (eds), *Papers from 30th* annual conference of the Standing Conference on University Teaching and Research in the Education of Adults (SCUTREA), 3-5 July, University of Nottingham: Continuing Education Press, pp 153-59

Hunt C (1999) 'Candlestick and faces: aspects of lifelong learning ', *Studies in the Education of Adults*, Vol 31, No 2, October, pp 197-209

Individual Learning News (2000) 'Helping in Schools', Summer p 19

IRB/International Adult Learners' Week 1999 (1999), Presentation of survey results from stage 1, ALW 1999 follow-up survey of Helpline callers

James K (2001) 'Prescribing learning', *Adults Learning*, April, p 3

Jennings L (1995) 'From student to tutor: learning through literature', in Preston P (ed) *Literature on Adult Education*, Nottingham, University of Nottingham

Johnston C (2000) 'Class and the Chardonnay set', *Times Education Supplement: FE Focus*, 28 July, p 11

Johnston R (2000) 'Education for inclusion or imprisoned in the global classroom?' in Jackson A and Jones D (eds), *Papers from 30th annual conference of the Standing Conference on University Teaching and Research in the Education of Adults* (SCUTREA), 3-5 July, University of Nottingham: Continuing Education Press, pp 173-181

Johnston R and Croft F (1998), 'Mind the gap: widening provision, guidance and cultural change in higher education' in Preece, J. (ed) with Weatherald C and Woodrow M (1998), *Beyond the boundaries: exploring the potential of widening provision in Higher Education*, pp11-19, Leicester: NIACE

Jones K and Swanton P (2000) 'Cool Work', *Adults Learning*, October, pp 21-23

Joseph Rowntree Foundation (1996), *Further Education for people with learning difficulties*, Social Care Research Findings 85

———— (1998) *Continuing education and equal opportunities for adults with learning difficulties*, Social Care Research Findings N18

Jude C (2001) 'The Citizens' Conference', *Adults Learning*, September, pp 12-14

Kennedy H, QC (1997) *Learning works: Widening participation in further education*, Coventry: Further Education Funding Council.

Lavalle I and Finch S (1999), *Pathways in adult learning*, Research Report 137, DfEE Publications

Lochrie R (2001) 'Pre-Election Perspectives', *Adults Learning*, March, p 11

Mackney P (2000) 'Time to take lazy employers to task for training', *Times Educational Supplement: FE Focus*, 27 October, p 36

Maguire M, Maguire S and Felstead A (1993) *Factors influencing individual commitment to learning: a literature review*, Employment Department Research Series No. 20, Sheffield: Employment Department

Malcolm J (2000) 'Joining, invading, reconstructing: participation for a change?' in Thompson J (ed) *Stretching the academy*, pp 12-22, Leicester: NIACE

Martin I (1999) 'Adult education, lifelong learning and active citizenship', *Adults Learning*, October, pp 16-18

———— (2000) 'Contesting citizenship', *Adults Learning*: special millennium issue, Summer, pp 12-14

———— (2001) *A note of fashionable dissent: Rediscovering the vocation of adult education in the morass of lifelong learning*, paper presented to the 2001 SCUTREA conference

Martinez P (2001) *College Improvement: the voice of teachers and managers*, London: LSDA

Maxted P (1999) *Understanding Barriers to Learning*, London: Campaign for Learning

Mayo M and Collymore A 'Widening participation through action learning in the community' in Thompson J (ed) *Stretching the Academy*, Leicester: NIACE

McGivney V (1990) *Education's for other people: Access to education for non-participant adults*, Leicester: NIACE

———— (1991) *Evaluation of the Women's Education Project in Belfast*, Belfast: Women's Education Project/Leicester: Leicester: NIACE

———— (1992a) (ed) *Opening colleges to adult learners*, NIACE, 1992. Leicester: NIACE

———— (1992b) *Motivating unemployed adults to undertake education and training*, Leicester: NIACE

———— (1993) *Women in education and training: Barriers to access, informal starting points and progression issues*, Leicester: NIACE

———— (1994) *Wasted potential: Training and career progression for part-time and temporary workers*, Leicester: NIACE

———— (1996) *Staying or leaving the course: Mature student completion and non completion in further and higher education*, Leicester: NIACE

———— (1997) Evaluation of the Gloucester Primary Health Care Project (unpublished), Gloucester, GLOSCAT

———— (1997a) *Develop the worker, develop the business: A guide for smaller businesses*, Leicester: NIACE

———— (1998a) *Excluded men: Men who are missing from education and training*, Leicester: NIACE

———— (1998b) *Adults learning in pre-schools*, Leicester: NIACE

———— (1999a) *Informal learning in the community: A trigger for change and development*, Leicester: NIACE

———— (1999b) *The contribution of pre-schools to the community*, PSLA/NIACE

———— (1999c) *Returning women: their educational experiences and needs*, Leicester: NIACE

———— (2000a) *Recovering outreach: Concepts, issues and practices*, Leicester: NIACE

———— (2000b) *Working with excluded groups*, Leicester: NIACE

———— (2001) 'Informal learning and bridging the class divide in educational participation', *Rising East*, Vol 4, No 2, pp 38-52

McGivney V and Thomson A (1995) *Foundation training: responding to labour market change*: a report commissioned by Coventry City Council City Development Directorate, Coventry City Council

Merrick N (2000) 'Refugees queue up for courses', *Times Educational Supplement: FE Focus*, 6 October, p 33

Merton B (1998) *Only connect*, Leicester: NIACE

Merton A (2001) *Thematic review of local education authority adult learning plans*, Leicester: NIACE

Midwinter E (1971) 'Educational Priority Areas: the philosophic question', Liverpool Educational Priority Area Project, quoted in Whaley, P (2000) 'Missionary and other positions: the community, the university and widening participation', in Thompson, J (ed) *Stretching the academy*, pp 125-140

Morrison T R (1995) 'Global transformation and the search for a new educational design'. *International Journal of Lifelong Education* 14, pp 188-213

Munn P, Tett L and Arney N (1993) *Negotiating the labyrinth: Progression opportunities for adult learners*, SCRE Report No 47, Edinburgh: the Scottish Council for Research in Education

Nash I (1999) 'Go local for learning', *Times Educational Supplement*, 23 July, p39

National Advisory Group for Continuing Education and Lifelong Learning (NAGCELL) (1999) *Creating learning cultures: Next steps in achieving the learning age*, second report of the National Advisory Group for Continuing Education and Lifelong Learning

National Committee of Inquiry into Higher Education (NCIHE) (1997) *Higher Education in the Learning Society*: Report of the National Committee ('The Dearing Report'), London: HMSO

National Institute of Adult Continuing Education (NIACE) (1999) Briefing on the Government White Paper, *Learning to succeed*, Leicester: NIACE

National Institute of Adult Education (NIAE), 1970, *Adult education: Adequacy of Provision*, London: NIAE

National Task Group for Widening Participation (2000), *Ideas for inclusion: an A to Z for practitioners*, published with the support of HEFCE

The Nestlé Family Monitor (2001) *Lifelong learning*, Study 504

Organisation for Economic Co-operation and Development (1997) *Literacy skills for the knowledge society: Further results from the International Adult Literacy Survey*, Paris: OECD

——— (1999) *Overcoming exclusion through adult learning*, Paris: OECD.

Osborne M, Cloonan M, Morgan-Klein B and Loots C (2000) 'Mix and match? Further and higher education links in post-devolution Scotland', *International Journal of Lifelong Education*, Vol 19, No 3, May – June, pp 236-250

OFTEL (1996) *Universal telecommunications services: a consultation paper*

Owens T (2000) *Men on the move: a study of barriers to male participation in education and training institutions*, Dublin: Aontas

Parry G (1997) 'Access education in England and Wales 1973-1994: from second chance to third wave', *Journal of Access Studies*, Vol 11, pp 10-33

Payne J (2000) 'Learning on Account in Dorset', *Individual Learning News*, April/ May, p 5

Percy K with Barnes B, Graddon A and Machell J (1988) *Learning in voluntary organisations*, Leicester: UDACE

Piatt W (2001) 'A school sweetener', *Guardian*, 13 April, p 15

Preece J (ed) with Weatherald C and Woodrow M (1998), *Beyond the boundaries: Exploring the potential of widening provision in higher education*, Leicester: NIACE

Preece J (2000) 'Challenging the discourses of inclusion and exclusion with off-limits curricula', *A global colloquium supporting lifelong learning*, Open University, Festival of Lifelong Learning, UEL, Open University and University of East London http://www.open.ac.uk/lifelong-learning

Price L (2001) 'Pre-Election Perspectives', *Adults Learning*, March, p 12

Queen Mary and Westfield College (1999) *Student Voice* Issue 1, The Widening Participation Collaborative Project of City University, University of East London, London Guildhall University, University of North London, the Open University in London, Queen Mary and Westfield College, London: Queen Mary and Westfield College, University of London

Rees G, Fevre R and Furlong, J (1997) 'History, place and the learning society: towards a sociology of lifetime learning' *Journal of Education Policy*, Vol 12, No 6, pp 485-497

Reynolds S (2001) 'Credit, quaifications ad the single framework for learning in Wales, *Adults Learning*, March, pp 23-24

Robertson D (1997a) 'The University for Industry – A flagship for demand-led training, or another doomed supply-side intervention?' *British Journal of Education and Work*, Vol 11, No 1, pp 5-21

———— (1997b) 'Growth without equity? Reflections on the consequences for social cohesion of faltering progress on access to higher education', *Journal of Access Studies*, Vol 12, No 1, Spring, pp 9-31

Robinson L (2000) 'Update on learning accounts', *Individual Learning News*, April-May, p 4

Robinson P (2000) 'Labour's post-16 failure', *The College Manager*, p 37

Rockhill K (1996) 'Challenging the exclusionary effects of the inclusive mask of adult education', *Studies in Continuing Education*, Vol 18, No 2, pp 182-93

Ronayne T (2000) Reaching the excluded, unpublished conference paper cited in Owens T (2000) *op cit*

Rubenson K (1998) *Adult readiness to learn: Questioning lifelong learning for all*, in Proceedings of the 39th US Annual Adult Education Research Conference, University of the Incarnate Word, San Antonio, pp 257-62

———— (1999) 'Sweden: The impact of the politics of participation', in Belanger P and Valdivielso S, (eds) (1997), *op cit*, pp71-94

Ryan, A (2000), 'Peripherality, solidarity and mutual learning in the global/local development business' in Thompson J (ed) *Stretching the academy*, Leicester: NIACE, pp36-53

Sand B (1998) 'Lifelong learning: vision, policy and practice', *Journal of Access and Credit Studies* Vol 1, No 1, Winter, pp17-39

Sanders C (2000) 'Bars to study cause offence', *Times Higher Education Suplement*, 11 August p6

Sargant N (2000), *The learning divide revisited*, Leicester: NIACE

Sargant N with Field J, Francis H, Schuller T and Tuckett A (1997) *The learning divide*, Leicester: NIACE

Sargant N and Tuckett A (1997) *Pandora's Box? Companion Papers on Motivation, Access and the Media*, Leicester: NIACE

Schuller T (2000) *Exploiting social capital: Learning about learning*, inaugural lecture at Birkbeck College, 9 February, Leicester: NIACE

Select Committee on Education and Employment (1999) *Access for all? A survey of ost-16 participation*, First Special Report, London: House of Commons
Select Committee on Education and Employment (2001) *Access to Higher Education*, London: House of Commons

Shaw M, Thompson J and Bane L (2000), 'Reclaiming common purpose', Editorial, *Adults learning* special millennium issue, Summer, p 5

Smith J and Spurling A (1999) *Lifelong learning: Riding the tiger*, London: Cassell

Smyth A (1997) 'Moving forward in strength and solidarity: Forging links between university and community-based women's studies initiatives in Ireland', proceedings of the UACE 1997 Annual Conference, quoted in Whaley, P (2000) 'Missionary and other positions: the community, the university and widening participation', in Thompson J (ed) *Stretching the academy*, pp 125-140

Soulsby J 'Learning in the fourth age', *College Research*, Winter 2000, London: Learning and Skills Development Agency, pp 23-4

Steele T (1999) 'Access, but not as we know it', *Adults Learning*, March, pp 22-24

———— (2000) 'Common goods: beyond the new work ethic to the universe of the imagination', in Thompson J (ed) *Stretching the academy*, pp 54-67

Stuart M (2000) 'Beyond rhetoric: Reclaiming a radical agenda for active participation in Higher Education' in Thompson J (ed) *Stretching the academy*, pp 23-35

Taubman D (2000) *Aylesbury revisited: Outreach in the 1980s*, pp v-ix, Leicester: NIACE

Taylor R (2000) 'Concepts of self-directed learning in HE: Re-establishing the democratic tradition' in Thompson J (ed) *Stretching the academy*, pp 68-79

Taylor S (2000) *Back on track: Successful learning provision for disaffected young people*, London: LSDA

Thomas L and Quinn J (2001) Commentary: Recent reports about higher education from the UK Select Committee on Education and Employment, *Widening Participation and Lifelong Learning*, Vol 3, No 1, pp 5-7

Thompson J (ed) (2000) *Stretching the academy*, Leicester: NIACE

Thompson J (2001) *Rerooting lifelong learning: Resourcing neighbourhood renewal*, Policy Discussion Paper, Leicester: NIACE

Thomson A (2001) 'MPs hear harsh loan truths', *Times Higher Education Supplement*, 2 February, p 3

Thomson A and Tysome T (1998) 'Cost forces out over-25s', *Times Higher Education Supplement*, 13 February.

Tight M (1998) 'Bridging the learning divide: The nature and politics of participation', *Studies in the Education of Adults*, Vol 30, No 2, October, pp 110-119

Times Higher Education Supplement (2000), *Opinion*, 11 August, p 14

Times Higher Education Supplement (2001) 'Mergers mean bigger but not always better', 19 January, p 14

Tonks D (1999) 'Access to Higher Education 1991-98: using demographics', *Widening Participation and Lifelong Learning*, Vol 1, No 2, pp 6-9

Tuckett A (2001) 'Countryside loses out in learning vision', FE-Focus, *Times Educational Supplement*, January 19, p.28.

———— (2001a) *If I can't dance – conviviality and adult learning*, lecture given at University of East London, 24 January

———— (2001b) 'Rostrum', *Guardian Education*, February 6, p 45

———— (2001c) 'Finally, a grown-up approach to adult learning', *Times Education Supplement: FE Focus*, 16 February, p 26

Tuckett A and Sargant N (1999) *Marking time: The NIACE survey on adult participation in learning 1999*, Leicester: NIACE

Turner C (2000) 'Where wings take dream', Commentary, *Adults Learning*, November, p 6

———— (2001) *Squaring the circle: Funding non-accredited adult learning under the Learning and Skills Council*, Leicester: NIACE

Tysome T (2000a) 'Extra millions fund a fifth of students', *Times Higher Education Supplement*, 28 July, p 4

———— (2000b) 'Doors still closed to ethnic minorities', *Times Higher Education Supplement*, 29 September, p 6

Uden T (1996) *Widening participation: Routes to a learning society*, Leicester: NIACE

UK Select Committee on Education and Employment. 2001, *Report on access to Higher Education*: 4th Report, London: House of Commons, February

Utley A (2001) 'Dropout rates don't reflect quality of provision', *Times Higher Education Supplement*, 6 April

Valentine T (1997) 'The United States of America: the current predominance of learning for the job', in Belanger P and Valdivielso S (eds), (1997), *op cit*, pp 95-108

Ward K and Steele T (1999) 'From marginality to expansion: An overview of recent trends and developments in widening participation in England and Scotland', *Journal of Access and Credit Studies* Vol 1 No 2, pp 192-203

Warwick D (2001) 'Integrating approaches to widening participation', *Update on Inclusion*, Issue 3, Spring, pp 5-7

Watson A and Tyers C (1998) *Demonstration outreach projects: Identification of good practice*, Final Report: national overview with individual project reports, SWA Consulting.

Whaley P (2000) 'Missionary and other positions: The community, the university and widening participation' in Thompson, J (ed) *op cit*, pp 125-40

Woodrow M (2000a) 'Lifelong learning to combat social exclusion: policies, provision and participants in five European cities', *Widening Participation and Lifelong Learning*, Vol 2, No 2, August

———— (2000b) *Putting a price on a priority: Funding and inclusive HE*, paper presented to UACE seminar on inclusion, Cambridge: UACE

———— (2001) 'Politics not paper: Why monitoring matters for widening participation projects', *Update on Inclusion*, Issue 3, Spring, pp 8-10

Workers' Educational Association (1998) *Bringing down the barriers: First WEA submission to the Learning Age Consultation*, London, WEA, the National Association

Working Brief (2000) 'Post-16 learning off target', November, p.3

Working Brief (2001a) 'Proposed reform to 16 hour rule still falls short', February, p 16

Working Brief (2001b) April
(a) front page, p 1
(b) 'EMAs increase participation in education', pp 14-15
(c) 'Provider base set to change' April, pp 16-19

Yarnit M (2000) 'Start with basic skills: A strategy for lifelong learning', *Adults Learning*: Soapbox, November, pp 22-23

More titles by Veronica McGivney

Informal learning in the community: A trigger for change and development
ISBN 1 86201 073 0, 1999, 112pp, £13.95
This report explores the role of community-based informal learning in widening participation and how to start people on a learning pathway. It identifies the kinds of services, structures and conditions needed to develop learning pathways and encourage people to make the transition from informal to more formal, structured and accredited learning.

'...may be read as an extended answer to the question posed in the recent White Paper, as to ways in which improvements in the delivery of adult learning can be secured...' (Reportback)

Recovering outreach: Concepts, practices and issues
ISBN 1 86201 099 4, 2000, 120pp, £14.95
This timely title explores the multiple understandings and connotations of the term 'outreach', the complex questions and issues involved in engaging with local communities and the very broad range of skills that this kind of work requires. It outlines the diversity of aims and practices in the different education sectors illustrating the varying importance attached to outreach work by different organisations and institutions.

'...particularly useful to [those] who often need to combine in one job tasks ranging from the most strategic...to the most operational.' (Learning and Skills Development Agency)

Working with excluded groups: Guidelines on good practice for providers and policy-makers in working with groups under-represented in adult learning
ISBN 1 86201 081 1, 2000, 32pp, £6.00
This publication shows the kind of approaches that work in making effective contact with people who do not consider learning a desirable or feasible option. Through this set of guidelines McGivney proposes some transferable 'principles of engagement' in working with excluded groups. A valuable resource for all those who wish to make educational opportunities available to those least represented.

'If you are at all interested in issues of inclusiveness and widening participation for adults, you will want to buy this book.' (Dr Paul Martinez, Raising Quality and Achievement Newsletter)

Returning women: Their training and employment choices and needs
ISBN 1 86201 057 9, 1999, 36pp, £6.00
A succinct overview of the issues facing women who wish to return to employment, education and training. Based on surveys and labour market studies, it examines:
- problems facing women returning to the labour market
- attitudes and barriers to training and employment
- types of training and education available to women
  returners.
This study shows that providing appropriate education and training for women returners is not just an issue of equality and social justice – it is also essential for the health of the national economy.

'...the study contains a wealth of information...it is clearly written, well presented and reasonably priced...for policymakers, educational providers and students on advanced studies of education.' (International Journal of Educational Development)

Excluded men: Men who are missin
ISBN 1 86201 039 0, 1999, 160pp, £14.9

Although surveys habitually show that more men than women are involved in post-compulsory education and training, this is largely accounted for by employer- and Government-supported training. Men with low literacy levels and few qualifications are under-represented in all forms of education and training. Social and economic trends suggest that the issue of male participation is a matter of urgency. This book looks at barriers to participation, implications for targeting and possible curriculum approaches, giving examples of effective practice.

'...play[s] a vigorous role in the process of reorienting and reinvigorating adult education.' (WEA Reportback)

Staying or leaving the course: Non-completion and retention of mature students in further and higher education
ISBN 1 87294 195 8, 1996, 224pp, £12.00

Using research findings and evidence from further and higher education, this book determines the scale and nature of student withdrawal. The author throws light on whether mature students are more likely to leave courses before completion and whether some groups are more at risk than others. The final section suggests strategies for dealing with the common reasons for withdrawal and for improving retention rates.

Adults learning in pre-schools
Published in association with the Pre-School Learning Alliance
ISBN 1 86201 040 4, 1998, 56pp, £6.00

This report investigates the extent and nature of uncertificated learning by parents who are involved in running pre-school groups. It is concerned with learning in the broadest sense of acquisition of transferable knowledge and skills, both personal and occupational, that may help people in any dimension of their lives.

Wasted potential: Training and career progression for part-time and temporary workers
ISBN 1 87294 149 4, 1994, 182pp, £9.95

A report showing how certain approaches often limit participation of part-time workers and those on temporary contracts. In contrast, examples of good practice demonstrate what can be achieved by employers who have designed and implemented imaginative programmes.

Develop the worker, develop the business: A guide for smaller businesses
ISBN 1 86201 031 5, 1997, 108pp, £25.00

A practical manual for those who want to initiate or improve staff training and development activities. There are facts and figures about small and medium-sized enterprises, flexible working and employer-provided training. This publication examines constraints and difficulties and the business case for training. It is illustrated by case study material.

These books are available from:
Publications Sales
NIACE
21 De Montfort Street
Leicester LE1 7GE
or order online: www.niace.org.uk